GOD IS IN THE CRAZY

Scripture quotations are taken from

The Holy Bible, New International Version®, NIV®

Copyright © 1973, 1978, 1984, 2011 by Biblica, Inc.™

Used by permission. All rights reserved worldwide.

Printed in the United States of America

Print ISBN: 979-8-89786-010-4

eBook ISBN: 979-8-89786-011-1

First Edition

Cover design & interior design by Pinpoint Publishing

Pinpoint PUBLISHING

Atlanta, GA
www.Pinpoint.pub

DEDICATION

To God, who gets all the glory for this whole thing.

We're not the masterminds. He is.

To our girls—Madison, Macy, Mackenzie and Madelyn

You've been on this journey with us from the start.

You've seen God move.

You've witnessed miracles.

You've walked with us through the hard stuff.

We are so proud of you—

But even more proud of your love for Jesus and His Church.

You four are the *WIN* for us.

To our new sons—Cadyn and Josh

Welcome to this crazy family!

We love you guys big time.

And to our little guy, Lincoln James

You made us Mimi and Pops, the best job we've ever had.

CONTENTS

FOREWORD 5

INTRODUCTION 9

ONE STORY, TWO VOICES.................15

SAY YES...19

STICK WITH IT....................................43

STRETCH YOURSELF...........................69

BE REAL..97

BETTER TOGETHER 121

BELIEVE FOR GREATER....................151

FINAL WORD: LET'S GO! 167

ACKNOWLEDGEMENTS.....................169

RECOMMENDED READING.................175

ABOUT THE AUTHORS.......................177

FOREWORD

There are books that inspire, and then there are books that bear witness. What you hold in your hands is the latter—a living testimony of what happens when ordinary people say "yes" to an extraordinary God.

In a world driven by performance, polish, and perfection, the story found in these pages is refreshingly different. It is a story not of heroes, but of humility. Not of flawless plans, but of faithful obedience. It's about what happens when God calls, and a servant heart answers, "Here I am, Lord. Send me."

At its heart, this book is a declaration of the Gospel—played out not just in pulpits and pews, but in the messy middle of leadership, transition, loss, growth, waiting, and hope. It's about saying yes when the blueprint is unclear. About stretching into places that feel too big. About believing for more when your resources say less. And perhaps most poignantly, it's about leading with authenticity in a world obsessed with image.

David and Michele McLain don't just tell their story; they live it out in full view. With courage, vulnerability, and Spirit-led conviction, they take us on a journey of faith that will resonate with anyone who has dared to follow God into uncharted territory.

From the decision to move their church from a familiar but fading location to a barren field of potential, to the heartbreak of deep personal loss just days after celebrating a long-awaited victory, this story reminds us that faith isn't forged in comfort—it's forged in surrender. Like Abraham leaving his homeland for a place God "would show him," the McLains stepped out, unsure of the path but sure of the One who was calling.

And in that uncertainty, God proved Himself faithful.

You'll read about how a congregation said yes to God before knowing the outcome. How fasting and prayer preceded property acquisition. How setbacks weren't signs of failure, but setups for a greater miracle. How a failed land contract was redeemed by divine timing. These moments echo the truth of Romans 8:28—

that God truly does work all things together for the good of those who love Him and are called according to His purpose.

This book is a reminder that obedience is our responsibility, and the outcome is God's. That's not just a catchy phrase—it's a foundational truth of the Kingdom.

This isn't a leadership book filled with formulas. It's a faith book filled with stories that breathe. Real moments. Real struggles. Real surrender. And through it all, a very real God.

As you read, you may find yourself reflecting on your own journey. The crossroads you've faced. The promises you're still waiting on. The parts of your life God is asking to stretch. The places He's whispering for you to trust again. And maybe—just maybe—you'll be inspired to say "yes" once more.

Because the truth is, the Church doesn't move forward on the backs of perfect leaders. It moves forward on the faith of those willing to be stretched, willing to be real, and willing to go where Jesus leads—even if it costs them everything.

In Isaiah 54, the passage that frames much of this journey, we read the call to enlarge our tents, stretch wide, lengthen cords, and strengthen stakes. This prophetic picture isn't just about growth—it's about preparation. God doesn't stretch us to break us. He stretches us to expand our capacity—to carry more of His presence, to reach more people, and to walk more deeply in purpose.

The McLains' story is a living fulfillment of that promise.

But perhaps what's most moving is the quiet resilience in the waiting. Those 90 days without a buyer. The feeling of failure. The long nights questioning whether God had really spoken. We've all been there. But their choice to declare, "God's timing is perfect," even when it didn't feel like it—that is what faith looks like in the dark.

And faith in the dark is still faith.

This book isn't just for pastors. It's for dreamers, doers, builders, and believers. It's for anyone who has ever faced a closed door, a delayed promise, or a divine detour. It's for anyone who's ever had to lead while grieving, or serve while questioning, or speak life while still trying to believe it for themselves.

To read this book is to be reminded that God is not looking for ability; He's looking for availability. That our potential is released in the stretching. That our influence is magnified in authenticity. And that our obedience, even when it feels small, is seen by the One who multiplies loaves and fishes and mustard seeds of faith.

As you turn these pages, prepare to be encouraged. But more than that, prepare to be challenged. Because once you see how God moves through people who simply say "yes," it's hard to go back to playing it safe.

My prayer is that this book will ignite something in you. That you'll begin to see your waiting as sacred, your stretching as preparation, your pain as part of the process, and your "yes" as the key that unlocks the next chapter of your calling.

So go ahead. Read with expectation.

And when the time comes to choose faith over fear, vision over comfort, and authenticity over applause—may you hear the voice of the Spirit saying,

Stretch wider. Dig deeper. Go further.

And may your response, like theirs, be simple and powerful:

"Yes, Lord."

Chris Sonksen
Pastor/Author and Founder of Church Boom

INTRODUCTION

If your story could bring God glory, would you tell it?

A few years ago, this simple question is what began prompting us to write this book. In our church, we regularly invite people to tell the story of their lives. Not just the highlight reel, but the outtakes, too. The broken dreams and the dreams-come-true. The bumps and bruises. The victory laps. The good, the bad and the ugly. In doing so, something crazy happens. Walls come down. Connections are made. Lives are changed. Simply by the sharing of a story.

Why? Because **stories** are **powerful** things.

Everyone loves a good story.

We are "wired" to listen, learn, and even *lean* into a good story.

That's why we scroll through Netflix, Hulu, Prime video, and other streaming sites, looking for a something to…

> capture our attention,
> take us for a thrill ride,
> hold us in suspense,
> or give us an "escape" from the everyday life we are living.

As we watch, without realizing it, we become strangely *invested* in these characters.

We follow them. We care about them. We root for them— or root *against* them.

Superheroes saving the universe.
Undercover government agents on top-secret missions.
Modern-day cowboys who own sprawling ranches.
Medieval warriors charging forward on violent battle-
fields.

That's what this book is. Our story.

It's a crazy story—and along the way, we have discovered
that God is in the crazy.

A LITTLE BIT ABOUT US

Allow us to introduce ourselves. We are David and Michele
McLain, an ordinary couple whom God called in 2003 to
become the new pastors of Central Assembly of God, a
historic church in Austin, TX. At the time of this writing,
nearly 22 years have passed since we first loaded up the
U-Haul and set out on the 6-hour drive south from our home
in Oklahoma City.

This book is our attempt to tell the story of what God has
done in our church—and in our own lives—during those 22
years.

We'll get to that in a moment, but first, let us share a little
more of our background:

David was a city kid who grew up in Dallas, TX.
Michele was from Beggs, a small town in rural Oklahoma.

David was from a small family—Mom, Dad, and his sister,
Barbara.
Michele had a large family—Mom, Dad, and six brothers:
Sean, Shane, Shannon, Scott, Matt, and Robbie. (*Yep, you
read that right. She was the only girl in a family of seven
kids.*)

David grew up singing in choirs and quartets.
Michele excelled in ballet dancing, running track and
basketball. (*More on that later...*)

At first glance, we were about as different as two people could be—but we had a lot more in common than you might think.

We both grew up in Christian homes, attended church every Sunday, and were actively involved in our youth groups. We both attended church camps in the summer, and it was there that we individually experienced the call of God upon our lives—and we both said yes. Even though we weren't pastor's kids, our lives centered around church—and we liked it that way.

Although we were from different states, our paths finally crossed on March 26, 1992. David was a sophomore in Bible college; Michele was a senior in high school, visiting the campus with her youth group. We met, of all places, at Whataburger in Waxahachie, TX. During our very first conversation—lasting no more than 20 minutes—we discovered that we shared the 3 essential ingredients for any lifelong relationship: Faith in Jesus, a love for basketball, and our shared admiration for the greatest player of all time: Larry Bird. (*That's pretty much all you need, right?*)

For the sake of time, we'll fast-forward through the next decade: We dated, married and started a family. God blessed us with four amazing daughters—Madison, Macy, Mackenzie and Madelyn. We have invested our entire married life (over 30 years now) into serving in the local church, which has been the highest honor of our lives.

Now for the crazy part…

OUR JOURNEY IN AUSTIN BEGINS

In November 2003, we were elected to serve as pastors of Central Assembly of God. We knew from the start our assignment would have its challenges. This 67-year-old church, established in 1938, found itself at a crossroads. It needed either a new location or a new vision. Perhaps both. As incoming pastors, we knew the church leadership would be looking to us to lead the transition. Change is never easy, and this church family was about to experience a lot of it. As expected, the transition was difficult in more ways than one. Financial setbacks. Staff turnover. Leadership tensions. Lack of clear direction. We will share many of those details throughout this book.

Now over two decades later, as we stand on the other side looking back, we can say without hesitation—even during the craziest of seasons, God was in the crazy.

Some would say we've done a difficult thing. There is some truth to that, we suppose. After all, we relocated an established church, bought and sold property, built two buildings, changed the church's name—and somehow lived to tell about it. None of which had we ever done before. We were pretty much figuring it out as we went. Thankfully, we also experienced numerical and spiritual growth beyond anything we had ever dreamed. To God be the glory.

GOD IS THE HERO OF THIS STORY

Please don't miss this (*or as the kids say, "don't get it twisted"*):

We are *not* the heroes of this story—*GOD IS!*

(*A fact that should become clearer with every turn of the page.*)

In fact, much of this book is about the things we got wrong, more than the things we may have somehow gotten right. There were many times we found ourselves living by fear instead of faith.

We were too reluctant to take risks.

We were too slow to obey.

We stood too long at the water's edge before finally stepping into it.

Our pride kept us from reaching out for help.

Our insecurity kept us feeling alone.

What we didn't realize then—but we do now—is that during all those years, God was doing something *in us*...so that later on He could do something *through us*. Isn't that just like God? He works through the people we would never have chosen—then later on, there can be no question who gets the glory!

GOD LOVES USING NOBODIES

Paul's words in the first chapter of 1 Corinthians clearly describe the kind of people whom God chooses to call into His service.   As you read the passage below, take note of the clear contrast between what the world values and what God values.

> *26 Brothers and sisters, think of what you were when you were called. Not many of you were wise by human standards; not many were influential; not many were of noble birth. 27 But God chose the foolish things of the world to shame the wise; God chose the weak things of the world to shame the strong. 28 God chose the lowly things of this world and the despised things—and the things that are not—to nullify the things that are, 29 so that no one may boast before him. 30 It is because of him that you are in Christ Jesus, who has become for us wisdom from God—that is, our righteousness, holiness and redemption. 31 Therefore, as it is written: "Let the one who boasts boast in the Lord."*
> *(1 Corinthians 1:26-31)*

There are two categories of people described above: *somebodies* and *nobodies*.

Of course, we probably all want to be considered wise, influential, noble and strong.

In other words, the *somebodies*.

But instead, God chooses to use the foolish, weak and despised.

You guessed it, the *nobodies*.

That's just the way of the Kingdom. God does great things through nobodies—but He will never share the credit. Nor should He have to. He created us from nothing. He called us from nowhere. Yet for some reason known only to Him, He chooses to use us for His glory.

The two of us—David and Michele—know better than anyone which of the categories above we fall into. We are weak, foolish, and unqualified. There is nothing for us to boast in, except for the goodness of God! To be clear, we know we have not "arrived." In many ways, it feels like we are just beginning. However, we have learned some lessons along the way—both what to do, and what not to do—and those are the insights we hope to share with you in these pages.

Lastly, this book isn't just about *our* **story. It's also about** *yours.* As you read these pages, the Holy Spirit is going to be speaking to your heart about taking crazy steps of your own. That has been our prayer all along. So open your heart and listen closely. May you hear His voice clearly calling you into a new season of faith and obedience. And whatever He calls you to do, may your answer always be yes—even when it seems crazy.

Because God is in the crazy.

ONE STORY, TWO VOICES

Before we ever started this project, we knew God was calling us to *co-author* this book—just as we are *co-pastors* of our church. Once that decision was made, the next question was *how*? After some discussion, we decided the most authentic approach would be for you, the reader, to have the opportunity to hear each of our unique "voices" throughout the book.

To accomplish this, we've chosen to add headings throughout the text which say:

(DAVID:)

(MICHELE:)

Or

(US:)

We hope this helps you keep track of whose "voice" you're hearing (reading), and we trust it will enhance your reading experience.

After all, some parts of the story can only be told by Michele, because those perspectives are her own. Likewise, other parts can only be told by David.

The remaining content may not be specific to either one of us—so we'll just take turns "talking," as if we were spending an afternoon, getting better acquainted, while sitting at a corner table in your favorite coffee shop (*…which, come to think of it, may actually be where you are reading this right now*).

We are so excited to share our crazy story with you.

The coffee is ready, so let the conversation begin…

> "THE GREATEST OPPORTUNITIES
> IN YOUR LIFE WON'T COME
> WITH A GUARANTEE.
> THEY WILL COME WITH A
> WHISPER FROM GOD SAYING,
> 'TRUST ME...SAY YES.'"
> - MARK BATTERSON

CHAPTER ONE:
DAVID:

When we left Oklahoma City in 2003 and moved to Austin, Texas, we didn't have a full plan. We had a calling. That was it. We had just been elected to serve as pastors of Central Assembly of God Church, a historic congregation with a strong legacy of over sixty years in the city. Before accepting the opportunity, we had of course spent considerable time in prayer, but also sought out all possible information we could find regarding the health and history of the church we were about to lead. We wanted to make sure we did our due diligence, as any wise leader should do. Over several weeks, we spoke not only to the current board members, but also to former staff members, including the previous pastor.

These conversations gave us lots of helpful insight as we prepared for our future role. Founded in 1938, this congregation had grown from humble beginnings to become a solid church making a generational Kingdom impact. In its heyday, the church had boasted a Christian school, a ministry training center, a radio and television ministry, and even hosted a city-wide theatre company. Under the leadership of the previous pastor, the congregation had developed a strong vision for missions work, both in financial support and active participation. Everything we learned during that discovery process seemed encouraging, and rightfully so. By all accounts, this was a church with a legacy in the city, a healthy financial standing, a unified congregation, and a vision for sharing the Gospel throughout the world.

However, there was one piece of the puzzle which caught our attention. The previous pastor shared something which would undoubtedly have a huge impact on the church's future. During one of our conversations, I remember him putting it bluntly: *"This church is at a crossroads. Either it needs to relocate, or it needs to totally reinvent itself to better reach this community. Either way, something has to change. That will be your biggest challenge moving forward."*

The more he explained his reasoning, the more I understood the dilemma. Many of the people who attended the church presently had once lived in the neighborhood surrounding the church, but over the years, they had moved away to other parts of Austin. As their families had grown, many of them had sought lower housing prices and better schools which were widely available in the suburban expansion of Greater Austin. They still loved their "home" church, but the gravitational pull to their new neighborhoods was a real thing. Although many still commuted on Sunday mornings, it had become increasingly difficult to sustain midweek ministries in the church, not to mention outreach ministry opportunities.

CHANGE YOUR LOCATION, OR CHANGE YOURSELF.

Thus, the "crossroads" statement. This was a moment of clarity, to say the least. The church couldn't stay the same or it would decline—maybe even die. A bold choice had to be made. Either change the location or change the vision. There didn't appear to be any other options.

In addition to the changing congregational dynamics, the community itself was also changing as well. The fastest growing demographic in the church's zip code was the Hispanic population. For many, English was their second language, if they were fluent at all. It didn't take long to realize that what the community needed most was a vibrant, Spirit-filled Spanish-speaking church. Simply put, that wasn't us.

So again, the church was at a crossroads. Change your location, or change yourself. Even with that knowledge, we didn't make an immediate decision. We decided to wait, to seek, to listen.

The challenge of relocating a sixty-seven year old church is not for the faint of heart. I may have been a young naïve pastor, but even I knew that! (We've all heard the stories from sweet old church ladies of their "former pastors" who tried to make changes a little too fast. Let us all bow our heads for a moment of silence in their memory…)

Two and a half years later, we still hadn't made a choice about which path to take. It's not that we didn't believe a change was needed. We just didn't know how to do it. We kept "doing church" on Sundays, but gradually fewer people were coming. One by one, people started finding churches "closer to home." We kept planning community outreaches where people received our handouts, thanked us for our kindness, but never darkened the doors of our church. It's not that we didn't want to serve people who never attended our church—(because that would sound pretty shallow, huh?)—it was just frustrating that *no one* would give us a chance. I felt God had called us to pastor people, not just distribute school supplies. And yes, I know there is value in meeting felt needs, but we wanted to have the opportunity to disciple people…which is hard to do when they don't come to your church, and you can't even speak their language.

The frustration was growing. After two and a half years, we knew the time had come for us to make a decision. Pick a side. Choose which side of the crossroads we would take.

CHANGE OUR LOCATION, OR CHANGE OUR VISION.

We didn't have a blueprint, but we had a burden. God had long ago burned it into our hearts that we were to be a community church. But it had become undeniably clear that you can't have a *community* church if no one in the congregation actually lives in the community! Something had to change. The time was now.

In January of 2006, we sensed God calling us to forty days of fasting and prayer. We knew we needed clear direction for our next step. So we called the entire congregation to join us in fasting for God's direction to be made undeniably clear. I still remember the sense of excitement shared by the entire church family. We knew God would answer. There was expectancy in the air. During that time, we kept praying, "God, what are You saying? What does obedience look like here? Just show us what You want us to do, and we will obey." And that's when God answered...

One morning, while I was in Bible study and prayer, I stumbled across a passage in the book of Genesis. In fact, it was one simple verse which I had read many times before, but this time was different:

> *"The Lord had said to Abram, 'Leave your country, your people and your father's household and go to the land I will show you.'" (Genesis 12:1)*

Suddenly, I felt it deep in my spirit—this wasn't just a story from long ago. This was personal. God was saying, just like He did to Abraham, "GO." Not "go with a plan," or "go when it makes sense," but *"go and I will show you."* In that moment, it became crystal clear that God was asking us to move. To trust Him without clarity. To obey without certainty.

It was right there in black and white—for Abram and for us:

> *Leave and go to a land I will show you.*

Just like that, we knew what God was calling us to do. He had answered. He had given us a divine imperative. So, now what? There was only one thing left to do: **SAY YES.**

It was a really cool moment when we shared with the leadership team what God had spoken to us, and they received it wholeheartedly. In fact, one of the elders in the church who had been very reluctant about the possibility of relocation had his own "word from God." He told me with tears in his eyes, "Pastor, I don't see where God is moving us, but I believe He's just getting us out of the way, because He has big plans for this building. All I know is that some other church is supposed to have this place, so we need to leave!" This was just another confirmation that God had spoken— and I needed all the confirmation I could get!

IT'S TIME TO MOVE

Relocating our church was a wild step. We were young—I had just turned 30, and Michele was in her late 20s—so we were definitely walking into uncharted territory. Neither of us came from pastoral families. We didn't have mentors walking us through how to sell a church building or how to relocate an entire congregation. We were walking in faith and learning on the go, with little more than conviction and prayer to lead us.

One day, I received a call from one of our board members who said, "Pastor, I think I found some property that would be great for our new church home. If you have some time this evening, let's go for a drive. I'd like you to take a look." Later that night, we pulled up to a 73-acre piece of land that appeared to be in the middle of nowhere. There was nothing about this place that screamed, "Future Home of YOUR CHURCH." The land was just an overgrown cow pasture with an abandoned farmhouse that seemed like it belonged in a haunted house movie.

The site was technically located outside of the city limits, just south of Hutto, north of Pflugerville, and east of Round Rock. It was *in* none of these cities, but *near* all of them. Looking back, the location was absolutely perfect for the coming growth that was still over a decade away—but I'm getting ahead of myself. On that random Tuesday night in 2006, there was nothing about this location—or this plan—that made sense on paper. The land was hard to find. The roads around it were filled with potholes. There were no utilities attached to the property. Not to mention the (somewhat important) detail that we didn't have the money! All that being said, from the first moment we stood on that land and prayed, we sensed the Holy Spirit saying, **"One day, this will be your home."**

Believe it or not, the asking price for the property was listed at $1.7 million for 73 acres. (Let that sink in a minute. That's a lot of land for a relatively small amount of money! The problem is we just didn't have any money.)

In spite of that little detail, we placed an offer on the land… and (drum roll please) they accepted our offer! Although we had already listed our existing building for sale—along with 4 acres of land in Central Austin—there were no potential buyers even showing interest. So we had no buyers, but we had faith. We had unity. We had peace in knowing that God had spoken, and we had obeyed.

MOVING FORWARD WITHOUT ALL THE ANSWERS

We moved forward, believing God would meet us in motion. According to the standard real estate contract, after signing the contract we had a 90-day feasibility period to either close the contract or void the deal. Our challenge was to sell our current building (which would give us more than enough money to buy the new property) or raise the funds some other way. So we did the only things we knew to do. We prayed. We worshiped. We fasted. We did "Jericho marches" around those 73 acres in the country, asking God to give us the land. (Of course, we only did those prayer walks in the daytime—nobody wanted to go anywhere near our little haunted farmhouse after dark!)

During this time, our church family came together around this vision—and it was beautiful to see parents bringing their children to see the land. Grandparents prayer-walking with their grandkids. Generations dreaming, praying and believing together. Seeds of faith were sown in the soil of those fields. We knew that would bear fruit—but when?

Before we could blink, that first 30 days flew by. There were no potential buyers for our building and no progress with our search for funding. We called lots of banks, explored (very creative) financing options, talked to our denominational lender, and even started believing for unexpected inheritances from rich uncles we didn't even know we had!

Soon the 60-day mark came and went…and still no progress. We had shared the vision with our church family, so we felt it was important to keep calling them back to prayer. So, each and every Sunday, I gave an update—which was pretty brief because *nothing* was happening—and then urged them to continue praying for God to make a way. I probably quoted every faith Scripture in the Bible at some point during those critical months. And yet, nothing happened. Not a single offer. Zilch. Crickets.

As the 90-day feasibility period drew to a close, I remember feeling pretty desperate. With only a week left, I knew that we needed a miracle now more than ever. There were a few "deals" floating around out there, I wondered if anything would materialize before the deadline? I will never forget when the clock struck midnight on the ninetieth day of the contract. (Yes, that probably sounds like a bad Cinderella reference, but I was literally waiting for my phone to ring, right up until the last minute.). No call came that night.

It was a Friday night…and Sunday was coming.

(Just to be clear, this is not some kind of cheesy Easter reference for all of you good Christians out there who are reading this book and expecting an "empty tomb" reference. Nope, this stone did *not* roll away. It just so happens that it was *literally* a Friday when our 90 days ran out...and the first thing that came to my mind that night was: "Oh no, Sunday is coming...and I have to explain this to everyone.")

STUMBLING THROUGH OUR YES

I didn't sleep well that night. Or the next. By the time I walked into church that Sunday, I felt like a complete failure. A fraud. A snake oil salesman who wandered from town to town, getting people's hopes up, and taking advantage of their simple trust. Clearly, this had never been my intention. I believed God was going to come through for us...but He didn't. At least not in the way I had hoped. I felt like such a fake. Maybe I had misheard God. Maybe I wasn't a good enough leader. Maybe I had led everyone down the wrong path. Now here we were standing at a dead end...and everyone was about to be looking at me saying, "But you said God had spoken to you."

Sometimes when I tell this story in a sermon, or in a conversation with other pastors, I make jokes about how I thought about running away that weekend. Maybe find a shade tree on the beach in Aruba. Or buy a one-way ticket to Greenland. Or just enroll our whole family in the "witness protection program" for disgraced pastors trying to find a new life off the grid. Any of these options would've looked pretty good that Saturday night! But in all honesty, this was no laughing matter. I was discouraged beyond words, and I knew that when morning came, I would have to stand before those people and explain. Something. Anything.

Truthfully, I don't remember a lot about that morning. It was all kind of a blur. After the praise and worship time, and the weekly announcements highlighting some upcoming church picnic or something...it was my turn to take the microphone. With a forced smile on my face trying to disguise my heavy heart, I shared the bad news: We didn't close the contract. The deal was off.

In that moment, I remember being fully aware that my next words would be critical—so I needed to choose them carefully. Would I whine about our situation, or would I reaffirm the sovereignty of God? By the way, you can't do both. You have to pick one. You can try to explain away your broken hopes and dreams, or you can exalt the One who holds the future in His hands.

I knew this was a pivotal moment for our church family— maybe even a turning point, though there was no way of knowing that at the time. As their pastor, I had to say something. So as I stood on that stage, I simply shared the one truth my soul was barely hanging onto: **"God's timing is perfect."**

(MICHELE:)

Here are some lessons we have learned (and are still learning) about both the challenge and the importance of saying YES:

1. FAITH DOESN'T WAIT FOR CERTAINTY

Sometimes faith feels like pretending. But it's not. It's holding onto what God said even when your emotions scream otherwise. It's being willing to look foolish in the natural while staying faithful in the spiritual. Faith isn't a feeling. It's a decision to trust God's voice more than your fear. More than your logic. More than the silence.

Looking back on that season, we now realize something profound: those 90 days weren't wasted. It was preparation. It exposed our insecurities and our desire for control. We had to learn to lead even when we were discouraged. To preach even when we weren't sure. To believe even when the facts didn't support the promise.

We like to say it this way: **Obedience is our responsibility, the outcome is God's.**

Through the years, this has become a guiding principle for us. Our job is never to produce results—it is to obey. God is the One responsible for bringing His promise to pass, in His way and in His timing.

Let's face it, faith is risky. It's disruptive. It tests your resolve. It reveals what foundation your life is built upon. But this journey with God—it's not built on certainty. It's built on trust.

Obedience doesn't start when things make sense. Obedience starts the moment you say "yes" to the One who called you.

And that "yes" will lead you places you never imagined—if you'll just keep walking.

2. GOD GROWS FAITH THROUGH WAITING

The 90 days we had to raise the money for the land in Hutto felt like both an open door and a ticking clock. We believed we'd hear back from banks. We expected real estate interest. We anticipated movement. And yet... we got silence.

Every day that passed without an offer chipped away at our confidence. We prayed harder, talked longer, and kept rallying our people. But with each "no," the waiting turned from uncomfortable to painful. There's a particular kind of pressure that comes when you've declared what God is going to do—and nothing is happening.

On day 90, there was no miracle check. No sudden phone call. Just disappointment. That Sunday, when David stood in front of our church fighting off a storm of emotions, he felt *exposed*. Like maybe he had misheard God. Like maybe he wasn't even meant to lead these people anymore. He felt—in his own words—not just discouraged, but **defeated**.

And yet, in the midst of that rawness, he was still able to declare, "God's timing is perfect." To be honest, in that moment he was preaching something he was still trying to believe. *(Have you ever been there? I know I have!)*

That moment wasn't about appearances. It wasn't about pretending everything was fine. It was about **leading in the dark.** About choosing to believe when believing was the hardest option on the table. Looking back, that was one of the most formative moments of our entire ministry. Not because we saw God move right then—but because we didn't.

Waiting reveals what's real in us. It strips away hype, performance, and shallow confidence—and replaces it with roots.

Waiting is the classroom where faith matures. It's where trust deepens and character forms. We thought the breakthrough was the blessing. But it turns out, the **waiting** was.

> *"But let patience have its perfect work, that you may be perfect and complete, lacking nothing."*
> *— James 1:4 (NKJV)*

There is a cost to waiting. It will confront your insecurities. It will test your theology. It will ask you, "**Is God still good if nothing changes today?**" And it will expose whether your trust is rooted in the outcomes—or in the nature of God Himself.

David and I had to wrestle with all of it. As young leaders, the weight of leading through disappointment felt enormous. We weren't just carrying our own hope—we were carrying the hope of an entire church (or so it seemed.) When we were tempted to rush ahead or "make something happen," God kept calling us back to stillness. To trust. To obedience.

That waiting not only stripped us of control, but also filled us with dependency. It reminded us that God's timing isn't just about schedules—it's about soul work. We weren't just preparing to *buy* land. Any business-minded person can do that. God was preparing us to *steward* it.

At the same time He was developing us, He was also preparing our people. Our waiting became their witness. They saw us doubt, pray, believe again, and keep walking. That transparency—our vulnerability in the waiting—became a testimony all by itself. We learned that sometimes what people need most isn't a flawless leader, but a **faithful** one.

Hear it again: **"Obedience is our responsibility. The outcome is God's."**

Waiting is not wasted time. It's the space where God grows deeper faith in us. It's easy to believe when everything is moving. But the real test of faith comes when everything is still.

> *"But those who wait on the Lord shall renew their strength;*
> *They shall mount up with wings like eagles,*
> *They shall run and not be weary,*
> *They shall walk and not faint."*
> *— Isaiah 40:31 (NKJV)*

In the waiting, God teaches us to stop relying on outcomes and start leaning into His voice. And maybe the greater miracle isn't what you're waiting for—but who you become while you wait.

3.   THE NEXT GENERATION IS WATCHING

(DAVID:)

In the weeks following the crushing disappointment of the 90-day waiting period, we were still holding on. Barely. The questions hadn't gone away. We were still trying to believe

God was in this—still choosing to trust, even though our faith felt thin.

One afternoon at home, Madison, our oldest daughter who was around nine years old at the time, had a friend over. The girls were sitting at the kitchen island on bar stools, eating snacks and chatting—just being kids.

On the counter between them sat a small plastic container filled with dirt. It was from the land in Hutto—the 73 acres we had walked as a family and prayed over as a church. Remember those "Jericho marches" we talked about earlier? Well, during one of those many prayer meetings on the property, someone had made the suggestion that we grab some shovels, fill a bunch of little jars with dirt from our "promised land," and then distribute them to everyone in the church family, asking them to pray for a miracle! So that's exactly what we did.

OBEDIENCE IS OUR RESPONSIBILITY, THE OUTCOME IS GOD'S.

On each jar we placed a sticker with the following Scripture:

> "I will give you every place where you set your foot, as I promised Moses." (Joshua 1:3)

Of course, we didn't know what the outcome would be, but we wanted to mark that land with faith. The jars were a declaration that even if we didn't yet hold the deed, we were standing on the promise. One of those jars had made its way into our home and somehow landed on the kitchen counter that day.

That's when Madison's friend pointed to it and asked, "What's up with this jar of dirt?"

Without missing a beat, Madison simply responded like it was the most obvious thing in the world. "Oh, that's dirt from our church property."

(Now, in that very moment...the dirt didn't legally belong to us, at all. Our contract had fallen through. So technically, I guess you could say that dirt was...
STOLEN! And not just the jar sitting on our kitchen counter. All of the dirt... in all of the jars...which had been scattered all across the Greater Austin area—it was all stolen dirt. But sweet little Madison didn't know that, and I certainly wasn't going to be the one to tell her.)

WORDS HAVE POWER

Her words had power. No hesitation. No apology. Just child-like belief.

I looked up from where I was sitting nearby, and in that moment, everything stopped. My heart caught in my throat. It wasn't just what Madison said—it was how she said it. With absolute confidence. With zero doubt. Her words carried more than information—they carried *faith*.

Here I was, carrying the weight of disappointment, questioning my ability to hear God, wondering why He hadn't come through for us. Basically, just having a grown-up pity party. Yet in that simple, offhand moment, my nine-year-old daughter reminded me of a truth I desperately needed to hear: **God is still in this.** And maybe even more, she reminded me that faith doesn't have to be complicated to be real.

Sometimes the next generation carries a level of faith we've forgotten in the trenches of leadership.

Madison wasn't making a prophetic declaration. She was simply stating what she believed to be true—because she'd seen us believe, and that belief had taken root in her. She believed because she'd watched us walk the land, pray over the property, speak about God's promise. And now, her words carried the echo of everything we had modeled— *even when I had seemingly forgotten it myself.*

That jar of dirt, sitting between two little girls eating goldfish in the kitchen, somehow became much more than that. It was a burning bush. It was God speaking once again to a discouraged dad who felt forgotten in his own personal wilderness. That jar of dirt reminded me that day that what we do as leaders and parents isn't just for us—it's for those coming behind us.

The next generation will build their faith on how we walk through uncertainty, not just how we celebrate victory.

We learned that legacy isn't something we write later—it's something we're already living. Every choice Michele and I made to speak life, hold onto hope, and keep prayer-walking the land one more time—collectively, choices were forming something strong in those little hearts who were watching us. Then one day when *they* face a season of silence, our hope is that they'll remember how we waited, trusted, and believed. We must remember that faith isn't just passed down in sermons; it's transferred through presence. Through perseverance. Through prayer in the waiting.

The next generation is watching, not just to learn what we believe—but to see if we actually live it. And if we will let them walk beside us—not behind us, not at a distance, but *beside* us—they'll not only carry the vision forward…they'll sometimes remind us why we had it in the first place.

> *"Truly I tell you, unless you change and become like little children, you will never enter the kingdom of heaven."*
> — *Matthew 18:3 (NIV)*

4.   GOD'S TIMING IS PERFECT...AND HE PAYS INTEREST

(MICHELE:)

A few weeks after Madison's childlike faith moment in the kitchen, something began to shift. It wasn't dramatic. It wasn't immediate. But there was a renewed sense that breakthrough was coming.

And then—it came.

We finally received an offer on our building, and we accepted it! After months of silence and struggle, the doors finally began to open. The momentum we'd been praying for started to build. There were still questions, still steps to take—but something had broken loose in the Spirit.

Once we had a pending contract with our own buyer, the first thing we did was reach out to our realtor to see if the 73 acres were still available. (*I bet you already know the answer to that one. Surely the land we had lost wouldn't still be available, right? I mean that would be CRAZY!*) Sure enough, the land was still on the market months later. So we made another offer, but this time instead of $1.7 million, we offered $1.6 million. Much to our surprise, the seller accepted!

God didn't just fulfill the promise. He **refined** us in the waiting—and then **rewarded** the wait. It was like He gave us a glimpse of what *He'd been doing all along*, behind the scenes. His silence hadn't been absence. It was strategy. He was orchestrating something better than we could have forced on our own timeline. *God's delays are not denials— they're divine appointments with maturity, alignment, and sometimes... favor.*

Once again, **"Obedience is our responsibility. The outcome is God's."** In this case, God's outcome included not only provision… but *interest*! He didn't just give us the land; He made it abundantly clear *this was His work all along.* (Plus, the Lord apparently decided to throw in a $100,000 discount, just for our trouble!).

HIS PLAN IS ALWAYS BETTTER

Let me share one more detail of this crazy story—a miracle that had been over twenty years in the making. As we've explained, before we could ever buy the new land in Hutto, we had to sell our old land in Austin—and in God's perfect timing, we did. So you may be wondering: who bought the building we left behind? I'm glad you asked.

A vibrant Spanish-speaking congregation, named Iglesia El Shaddai, was the church family God hand-picked to move into our former home. Led by a passionate and visionary leader, Pastor Marivel Reyes, they offered a wide variety of weekly outreach ministries including ESL classes, financial training resources, literacy programs, and even a food distribution center. This was exactly what we had been praying for—a church that was uniquely called and qualified to make a difference in that neighborhood, better than we ever could've done.

This growing Spirit-filled church was already averaging around 500 in weekly attendance, and new people were joining each and every week. However, like many churches, their income was playing catch-up to their attendance, so purchasing our building was a huge step of faith for them. But still, they said YES—and on their very first Sunday in their new home, over 1,000 people showed up to celebrate their new beginning! What a beautiful confirmation of God's favor.

A TWENTY YEAR MIRACLE

How could this story get any better? I'm glad you asked.

As promised, here is the "miracle in the making" part of the story. Back in the early 1980's, a husband and wife had left their home in Mexico and made their way into the United States—more specifically, Austin, Texas. Like many immigrant families, life in a new place was difficult for them, but eventually they were able to find work and establish a home. Back in Mexico, they had lived under the strong influence of Catholicism, so religious practice was something they were acquainted with. However, neither of them had any personal understanding of the Gospel, and therefore no relationship with Jesus at all. That is until one Sunday when, for no apparent reason, they felt strangely drawn to attend a nearby church.

The name of the church was Central Assembly of God, and the pastor was a loving and energetic man named Tom Wilson. The couple was still learning English, but they were able to understand most of what was shared that day. The Holy Spirit must have filled in the gaps, because when Pastor Wilson gave an invitation at the end of his message, this couple responded and gave their lives to Jesus! In the weeks that followed, their faith continued to grow, and soon they began inviting others to attend the church along with them. Because these new families spoke very limited English, the church launched a Sunday School class to be taught in Spanish, and the steady growth continued.

In time, it became evident that God was leading this small group of believers to start a church of their own. Because that first couple from Mexico had been so instrumental in growing and shepherding the group, they became the obvious choice to serve as its leaders. More specifically, it was the wife—*Marivel Reyes*—who stepped into the role as pastor of the church. So with Pastor Wilson's blessing, a new church was planted in the city.

Over the next two decades, this small group of believers grew to become a vibrant growing congregation named *Iglesia El Shaddai*. This is who God chose to buy our building! The same building where they started twenty years earlier. The same building where their pastor first encountered Jesus. The same building they occupy today, as they continue making Kingdom impact. What a miraculous full-circle moment. Crazy, huh?

God is always in the crazy. Looking back, it's as if He was saying, "Why did you worry? I had this all under control. I had *you*. And I had *them*. The delay wasn't punishment—it was positioning."

When you trust God's timeline, you get more than you expected—not just in resource, but in revelation. He lets you see how your obedience fits into His larger Kingdom strategy. And when He shows you *why* the waiting mattered, it's humbling. You realize that your YES wasn't just about your breakthrough—it was about someone else's, too. God didn't just fulfill His promise to us. He fulfilled His promise to that neighborhood. To the people we weren't called to reach—but someone else was. We stepped out with faith, and when it looked like nothing was happening, everything was. God was aligning timing, people, resources, and opportunities in ways we never could have orchestrated. And when the time was right, He opened the floodgates.

> ## IT'S AS IF HE WAS SAYING, "WHY DID YOU WORRY?"

God's timing is *always* perfect.

THE CHOICE IS YOURS.

This chapter isn't just a story about land, leadership, or church planting. It's a testimony to what happens when you say **YES** to God—before you know where it's going, or how it will work. Before you see the outcome. Before you feel ready. It's about surrendering to a whisper in your heart, not just the logic in your brain.

We've learned this: **Every move of God begins with a YES**. And often, that yes will lead you into territory that feels wild, uncertain, and way beyond your ability. But that's the whole point.

God is in the crazy.

He meets you in the faith that looks foolish. He moves in the silence that feels like absence. He forms you in the seasons where you feel most unsure. And when the story unfolds—when the breakthrough comes—you'll realize that the crazy wasn't chaos...it was God's *calling* for you to trust Him one more time.

Whether you're facing a decision, a delay, or a door you're scared to walk through, this is your invitation: **Say YES.**

PRACTICAL TAKEAWAYS

» **Your yes matters more than your readiness.**

God doesn't need your perfection—He's after your obdience..

» **The waiting isn't punishment—it's preparation.**

In the stillness, God is sharpening your character for the calling He's entrusted to you.

» **The next generation is learning how to say yes by watching you.**

Let them see your trust, not just your triumph. Let them see your wrestle—and your resolve.

» **God's timeline is strategic, and His outcomes are multiplied.**

When you trust Him fully, He not only fulfills the promise—He often pays back the waiting with interest.

REFLECTION QUESTIONS

Use these for personal reflection, couple conversations, or your leadership circle.

1. **What yes is God waiting for from you right now?**

2. **What "crazy" obedience have you been resisting because it feels impossible or unqualified?**

3. **In what area is God asking you to trust His timeline more than your own expectations?**

4. **How are you modeling a lifestyle of yes for those following you—your children, your team, your community?**

5. **Where can you look back and say, "God was in that crazy thing I never would've chosen—but I'm glad I said yes"?**

STICK WITH IT

> "I HAVE FOUND THAT THERE ARE THREE STAGES IN EVERY GREAT WORK OF GOD: FIRST IT IS IMPOSSIBLE, THEN IT IS DIFFICULT, THEN IT IS DONE."
> - HUDSON TAYLOR

CHAPTER TWO:

We thought the hard part was over.

After all, we had said YES.

We had fasted and prayed for God's direction. We stepped out in bold faith. We rallied our church family behind a fresh vision of the future. We sold our old building and found the perfect location for our new home. Even when our first contract fell through, we kept trusting in God to make a way...which, of course, He did. After all, His timing is perfect.

The second time around, our contract was a success. In fact, we got a $100,000 discount—and we even paid $1.6 million in cash. How cool is that? Surely, this transition would mark the beginning of unstoppable momentum. What could go wrong when God was so clearly with us?

But here's the thing about following God: saying **YES** is only the beginning. The real test is whether you'll still say **yes** when the crowds leave, when plans stall, and when the dream looks more like a desert than a destiny.

This next chapter isn't about the thrill of launching—it's about the pain of enduring. It's the part of the story most people don't talk about. But we will. Because if we hadn't learned how to **stick with it,** we never would have seen what God had in store next.

ENDURANCE STARTS WHERE EXCITEMENT ENDS

(DAVID:)

Sunday May 6, 2007 was a day I will remember the rest of my life. We called it "Homecoming Sunday," but this wasn't just any old church picnic. This grand gathering was a highly-anticipated celebration of the 70th anniversary of our church family. Invitations had been mailed out to every former church member we could find an address for. Special guests would include three former pastors (Paul Joyner, Tom Wilson, and Roger Lewis), as well as the only founding member who was still alive, Bernice Polvado. "Sister Polvado," as she was known, had been the recording secretary in the very first business meeting, when the church began all the way back in 1937.

Slideshows had been prepared. Scrapbooks were on display, arranged by decades, much to the delight of all those who came to reminisce and reconnect with old friends. "Dinner on the grounds" would immediately follow the celebration service. Indeed, this was going to be quite the party.

One of the biggest highlights of the day was to be the first public announcement of the church's new name. Formerly known as Central Assembly of God, we would now officially begin operating as The Bridge Community Church. A new name. A new location. A new vision. This day would be the first time we publicly declared the new future of the church, and it would also be the last time we would ever be together in the place we called home.

The atmosphere was electric as people began filing in. There was laughter, warm hugs, and tears—lots of tears. The entire property was bustling with people from every generation of the church's history. Former choir members, Sunday School teachers, deacons, nursery workers, staff pastors and prayer warriors—they had all come home to the sacred grounds where they met Jesus and found a spiritual family.

In fact, it was not uncommon throughout that day to hear someone proclaim, "This is what heaven must be like!"

When we finally got the service kicked off, everything we had envisioned for the day went even better than expected. The corporate singing seemed almost angelic. The special recognitions were beautifully done. Each of the former pastors not only shared fond memories of days gone by, but also affirmed their heartfelt belief that the best days of the church were still ahead.

The culmination of the day was the invitation to join us (the very next week) for our first service in our new location, Brookhollow Elementary School, followed by a closing prayer of blessing.

The special day was rightly called a "Homecoming" – for that's exactly what it was. During that season, the average Sunday attendance of our church would've been somewhere around 200-225 people. But on this day, over 500 gathered together for the celebration. We had a packed house, to say the least! (…and what pastor doesn't love preaching to a packed house?) It was awesome. There was joy, vision, unity, and momentum. Indeed, it felt like confirmation from Heaven itself:

God is with us. The hard part is over. We're doing this! LET'S GO!!!

However, when the celebration service ended and people began saying their tearful goodbyes, the strangest thing started happening. Something I definitely did not see coming.

WHAT IS HAPPENING RIGHT NOW?!?

One person after another came up to Michele and me, gave us a hug, and said goodbye. There was nothing unusual about that. So we simply responded, "See you next Sunday!" Of course, we were referring to the first Sunday in the new location: Brookhollow Elementary School. After all, we had been preparing for months to transition into a "portable church." We had prayed, planned, purchased equipment, trained volunteers, and cast vision. We were ready. In exactly seven days, we would move into the next phase of the promise.

Surely, everyone was coming with us, right? Wrong.

One by one, these faithful church members hung their heads and delivered the bad news:

> "Umm, sorry Pastor, we really wanted to tell you before now, but this will be our last Sunday."

> "Pastor, we've been praying, and we feel God is calling us to another church."

> "We're really excited about this new vision for the church. It sounds great...but we're just not sure it's for us."

> "You know Pastor, that new location you're moving to is actually farther away from where we live, so we are going to start looking for someplace closer to home. We wish you the best though..."

And this last one really got to me:

> "When you build the new building, we'll definitely come back. But this whole setup and teardown thing? That's just not for us."

(I would love to say that Michele and I had only the purest Christlike thoughts when we heard those words above...but this is a non-fiction book. So, I'll just leave it to your imagination.)

Needless to say, our mood started shifting pretty dramatically during all those goodbye hugs. In just minutes, our confidence was shaken. We went from thinking our beloved church family was ready to follow us into this brave new world…to wondering whether or not anyone was going to come with us.

And then came the gut punch.

WHERE DID EVERYBODY GO?

That next Sunday, **only 60 people** showed up at the elementary school. Not 500. Not 225. Just 60. That Sunday didn't just feel disappointing—it felt devastating. We had just experienced unanimous excitement and support. And then, just like that, the crowd vanished. (What happened to that "heaven-on-earth" vibe?)

That was the moment when celebration collided with reality.

Perhaps the situation would have been easier to accept had our congregation not voted—*unanimously*, by the way—to take the steps we had taken thus far. If Michele and I had dreamed up all of this CRAZY stuff on our own, and then somehow tried to force our own agenda onto these poor, unsuspecting church members—I could understand if they were reluctant to get on board. But that was not the case. In fact, nothing could be further from the truth.

In those days, I was so determined to build consensus and protect unity that we brought every single decision to a congregational vote. We voted to put our building up for sale. We voted on the asking price. We voted to approve the buyer. We voted to pursue the 73 acres in Hutto. (*That one, we ended up voting on twice!*) We even voted on changing the name of the church. Like I said, we voted on *everything*! So how could the same people who *unanimously* voted to relocate the church suddenly decide *not* to come with us?

Whatever their reasons, that's what happened.

PRUNING IS PAINFUL...BUT NEEDED FOR GROWTH

The reality was crushing. We were hurt. Confused. Angry. We had followed God's voice, sold our building, stepped out in faith, and now we were pastoring a congregation that had decreased by 75%—seemingly overnight.

From time to time, Michele and I get randomly asked this question, *"Are you guys a church plant?"* We always laugh—not because it's funny, but because the answer is complicated. Technically, the answer is no. We didn't plant this church. It's been around for over 80 years now. That's quite a legacy.

We count ourselves honored to be building on the foundation laid by the thirteen pastors who came before us.

WE DIDN'T PLANT A CHURCH—WE NEARLY KILLED ONE.

Perhaps a more accurate answer would be: **We didn't plant a church— we nearly killed one.** As unintentional as it was, that's what happened. Almost. The breathing was shallow. The pulse was faint. But there was always a heartbeat. Then, by nothing less than God's mercy and grace, we were able to **revive** it.

It wasn't a launch. It was a funeral… followed by resurrection.

That was never our plan, but it became our story. And let us tell you—revitalization is not for the faint of heart. It's not glamorous. It's not filled with launch teams, countdown videos, or marketing hype. It's filled with *grit*. It's holding onto a vision when the room is empty. It's pastoring through heartbreak and disappointment. It's looking at your spouse and saying, "We're going to keep going," even when nothing in the natural makes sense. But this is what we've learned: when the lights fade and the crowd leaves, God is still there.

During what we call the "portable church" season, one verse that became our lifeline:

> *"Let us not become weary in doing good, for at the proper time we will reap a harvest if we do not give up." (Galatians 6:9)*

Those words weren't just motivational—they were oxygen to us. They reminded us that "the proper time" wasn't up to us. Our only job was to **stick with it.** To keep showing up when nothing looked like we had imagined—and still believe God is working.

I love how Paul uses the imagery of *harvest* in this passage. It's easy to understand this principle in the natural terms, because even a child can understand how God has hardwired the concept of "waiting" into his creation. When you plant a seed, you have to wait for it to grow. There is no shortcut to a harvest. No fast-forward button. No expedited service or overnight delivery. You simply have to wait for it.

So every Sunday, for two years, we just kept showing up. Preaching to 60 like we had 600. Worshipping through doubt. Leading through pain. Of course, this wasn't just Michele and me—there was a small, but faithful, core team of volunteers who "stuck with us" every step of the way. *(You know who you are, and we could never say "thank you" enough!)* Unloading trailers. Setting up sound systems. Stacking chairs. Hanging banners. Together, we understood we weren't building a church from scratch—we were trusting God to bring about a harvest...and He did. Not overnight. But at the proper time.

IT'S TIME TO TAKE A STEP

(MICHELE:)

After surviving two long years as a portable church, the day we left Brookhollow Elementary and moved into a leased space in the Windermere shopping center felt like an answer to prayer. We were no longer loading and un-loading trailers, setting up and tearing down, or navigating unpredictable school gym logistics. We had a key. A space. A home—even if it was tucked into a corner where no one could find us. *(If you know, you know.)*

It felt like progress. It *was* progress. But it wasn't the finish line. Thankfully, we owned 73 acres—the land we'd prayed over, walked around, and believed for. No doubt, God had given us our "promised land," but we didn't have enough money to build anything on the property. So, we remained in limbo – no longer portable, but still not permanent. Just in between.

At first, we thought it was a temporary delay. But the days turned into months, and the months into *years*. Seven years, to be exact. The miracle of selling our building and buying the land hadn't completed the story—it had only begun it. And that's when we learned a critical leadership truth: **just because God provides a miracle, that doesn't mean the work is over.**

God had done His part. Was He now waiting on us to do ours?

If that was the case, then we had a really big problem. In those days, to say that our leadership team was lacking clear direction on what to do next would be a massive un-derstatement! The board members were looking to David for a plan—but he had no idea what to do. We had never built a building before. So the longer we went without a plan, the more restless everyone was getting. Pretty soon, the ideas started flying in from every direction—but all of them were bad! (Sometimes the only thing worse than *no* plan…is a *bad* plan.) You name it, we heard it.

One board member wanted to put portable buildings on the property, like the kind that schools use for overcrowding. Another individual suggested we erect a shell of a metal building and start meeting in it immediately. After all, we could just finish out the interior later, when the money was available. I knew we were pretty much hitting rock bottom when another leader handed David a restaurant napkin with a floor plan scribbled on it! All of these people meant well, but they didn't know what they were doing—and neither did we!

> *JUST BECAUSE GOD PROVIDES A MIRACLE, THAT DOESN'T MEAN THE WORK IS OVER.*

In desperation, we hired an architectural firm to help us design a building. Unfortunately, the design he created would've cost over $6 million to build – which was completely out of our reach – so six months and $25,000 later, we were no closer to having a viable plan. Next, we hired yet another consultant, this time with a $75,000 price tag, who actually did help us put together a more achievable strategy, but its success was dependent on the sale of a portion of our land. So we signed a listing with a commercial real estate broker, but no buyers showed any interest. To make matters worse, the church finances had been steadily decreasing, so David had voluntarily taken multiple pay cuts in an effort to protect the staff.

To be honest, we were just tired.

Every door seemed closed. Every step we took seemed like a dead end. Confusion soon crept in. We were stuck. Disoriented. Wondering how the God who had moved so clearly before had now gone quiet.

STOP YELLING AND START STEPPING

More than once during that season, David and I felt like shouting, *"God, do You see us? Do You remember us? Did You forget what You told us? Are we still on Your radar?"* We weren't just praying—we were pleading. Crying out. Yelling into the silence. And for a while, it felt like that's all we could do. We were stuck between promise and possession, obedience and fulfillment. It was exhausting.

But then one night while I was spending time alone in prayer, I sensed something shift—not in my circumstances, but in my spirit. It was like the Holy Spirit whispered, *"It's time to stop yelling and start stepping."*

Immediately, I was reminded of the story of the Israelites crossing the Red Sea. In Joshua chapter 3, the people of God were poised to enter the land God had promised them. They had spent 40 years wandering the wilderness because of their lack of faith to trust God. As you may recall, Moses had sent twelve spies to scout out the land, and ten of them came back and spread fear among the people. Only Joshua and Caleb believed God could do what He promised. Fear won the vote, and Israel was sent into the desert.

Now, 40 years later, they stood once again in front of a body of water. The first time, it was the Red Sea. This time, the Jordan River.

> *"And the Lord said to Joshua, 'Today I will begin to exalt you in the eyes of all Israel, so they may know that I am with you as I was with Moses. Tell the priests who carry the ark of the covenant: When you reach the edge of the Jordan's waters, go and stand in the river.'" — Joshua 3:7-8 (NIV)*

That was God's big plan? Just stand in the water? But
Joshua was ready to say YES—even when it didn't make
sense.

While walking in Moses' shadow during all those years in the
wilderness, Joshua had been given a front row seat to the
power and provision of God! He had learned a thing or two
about the blessings of obedience and the consequences
of disobedience. Now, he was willing to trust God fully—
and he hoped the Israelites, as a whole, had learned their
40-year lesson, as well!

So without further delay, Joshua shared the plan with the
people, right down to the last detail. This strategy was
unconventional, to say the least, but Joshua had learned not
to hesitate when God says it's time to move.

> *"Now then, choose twelve men from the tribes of
> Israel, one from each tribe. 13 And as soon as the
> priests who carry the ark of the Lord—the Lord of all
> the earth—set foot in the Jordan, its waters flowing
> downstream will be cut off and stand up in a heap."
> (Joshua 3:12-13)*

What happened next was incredible, but it never would've
happened unless Joshua was willing to obey God's direction.

> *14 So when the people broke camp to cross the
> Jordan, the priests carrying the ark of the covenant
> went ahead of them. 15 Now the Jordan is at flood
> stage all during harvest. Yet as soon as the priests
> who carried the ark reached the Jordan and their
> feet touched the water's edge, 16 the water from
> upstream stopped flowing. It piled up in a heap
> a great distance away, at a town called Adam in
> the vicinity of Zarethan, while the water flowing
> down to the Sea of the Arabah (that is, the Dead
> Sea) was completely cut off. So the people crossed
> over opposite Jericho. 17 The priests who carried
> the ark of the covenant of the Lord stopped in the*

middle of the Jordan and stood on dry ground, while all Israel passed by until the whole nation had completed the crossing on dry ground. (Joshua 3:14-17)

Notice this simple fact: Nothing happened for Joshua and the Israelites until the priests *put their feet into the water.* The waters didn't part at the sound of their cries—they parted at the act of their faith.

We realized God wasn't just waiting for the right buyer or builder—He was waiting for **our next step**. He was calling us out of paralyzed frustration and into *activated faith*. It wasn't enough to *believe* the promise. We had to *move toward* it again. That moment became a dividing line for us. We shifted from waiting on God to partnering with Him. Less dramatic prayers, more decisive obedience. Less whining, more working. We began asking,

"What's the next bold, obedient step we can take— even if it feels crazy?"

THE TENSION IN THE TIMING

If you want to be someone who consistently endures during difficult times—who sticks with it—you're going to have to learn to be OK with *not always seeing the big picture.* Often things in life just don't make sense in the moment. Life is hard…and confusing. This is not only true for us today—as if life struggles are something new in the twenty first century—but, it has always been the case.

Throughout the Gospels, we clearly see how often Jesus' own disciples were frustrated by his lack of clarity. He spoke in confusing parables which had to be explained later. He avoided opportunities to promote himself as the new Messiah, choosing instead to stay under the radar for a while longer. He healed people, then told them not to talk about it. Not to mention he had this annoying habit of talking about leaving them one day soon—*that one really bothered them*—but He promised to come back to get them…eventually! They just had no idea when, so He told them to stay ready at all times. Crazy stuff!

In John 13, we see one of those moments play out right before us. Jesus had gathered his disciples to share the Passover meal together. During the meal, he surprised them all when he stood up from the table, took off his outer clothing, wrapped a towel around his waist, filled a basin with water, and started to washing the disciples' feet. *How strange*, they thought. This was something only a servant would do—but Jesus was their leader. The only disciple bold enough to say something in that moment was Peter. He stopped Jesus and asked for an explanation. This was the only answer he received:

> *"You do not realize now what I am doing, but later you will understand." (John 13:7)*

Jesus didn't explain further. He didn't clear up all the confusion. He didn't offer the view from 30,000 feet, to help them make sense of it all.

Just this: *" You don't understand now, but later you will."*

That was us in 2013! We could relate to the confusion of Peter. We shared his frustration with Jesus' lack of details. We were living in the "now" with very little understanding— and clinging to the belief that "*later* " it would make sense.

God wasn't just building a building. He was building *us*. This waiting period was a training ground for us. And the deeper truth? If we had received the promise any earlier, we probably wouldn't have been ready. He loved us too much to rush us. He was growing our capacity. He was deepening our roots. And He was reminding us—**this story was never going to be about our efficiency. It was always going to be about His glory.**

More of Him. Less of us.

THE WEARINESS OF WAITING

There's a kind of tiredness that doesn't come from lifting weights or running on a treadmill—those are physical. You can recover from them in a couple of days. Leading through times of uncertainty—now that's a whole different level of "tired." It's hard to keep showing up every day when the people are few, the resources are scarce, and the vision feels blurred. That's the kind of tired we lived with for years.

And the longer we waited for breakthrough, the more the weight of leadership pressed down. Key staff members moved on. Core families left—people we'd cried with, prayed with, built with. Some relocated. Some burned out. Others just couldn't see the vision anymore. Honestly, deep down inside, we understood. (Sometimes we wanted to leave, too!) Waiting is hard. But leading people *while* you're waiting is even harder.

Waiting can make you weary.

We were still holding onto the promise, but our hands were getting tired. And believe me, the temptation to quit was very real. Looking back, we asked each other more than once: *Why are we still here? Why didn't we walk away? Why didn't we start over somewhere new?*

But every time those questions rose up, so did two clear answers:

First, **we had made a promise to the people.** (We had sold their building…so we couldn't leave now. That's not the legacy we wanted to leave: *"Hey look, see that couple over there? They're the pastors who killed Central Assembly of God Church."*)

Second, **we trusted in the promise of God.** Even when we didn't feel it, we chose to believe He was still at work. Something was happening behind the scenes. Like Jesus told Peter, "You don't realize what I am doing now, but later you will understand."

So, what was the hold up?

Maybe the "holding pattern" wasn't just about contracts, or builders, or architectural plans.

Maybe there was something else at work.

Maybe we just didn't realize it yet…but we were about to.

Remember that incredible moment (in Joshua 3) when the Israelites had to step into the Jordan River before the waters parted? **The miracle didn't come from standing and waiting. It came when they *moved*. When they put their feet into the water.**

Maybe we weren't just supposed to pray for breakthrough— we were supposed to walk toward it. Maybe it was time to take another step. Maybe it was time to get our feet wet.

What we didn't know then was that our "next step of faith" wouldn't look like a miracle—it would look like a man named **Lonnie Huett**.

A MAN NAMED LONNIE

(MICHELE:)

In early 2013, David attended a fundraising golf tournament hosted by one of the missions organizations we support. During the awards dinner that night, one of the other golfers named Lonnie Huett walked up to David to introduce himself. With tears in his eyes, Lonnie said the strangest thing, "I know we've never met, but I feel like the Lord told me I'm supposed to work with you." It sounded crazy at the time, but since Lonnie seemed very sincere, David politely thanked him and suggested it might be a good idea for the two of them to meet for coffee in a few weeks. That was it. No burning bush. No signs and wonders. Just a coffee appointment.

When David came home and told me, I responded like any practical person would. I had a few questions, to say the least. *"Who is this guy? What does he want? Why are you meeting with him?"* David didn't really have many answers. He had found out that Lonnie was a pastor in the Fort Worth area—and because he was an older man, David thought maybe Lonnie was looking for a position on our staff, perhaps as our senior adults pastor.

I remember telling him, *"You know we don't have money to hire anybody. We're trying to build a church. You should just cancel that appointment—it's a waste of your time."* Still, David felt it was important to meet Lonnie for coffee anyway. So I decided not to argue with him about it—after all, what harm could one coffee appointment do anyway?

When the day arrived, Lonnie made the three-hour drive to Round Rock. The two of them grabbed a corner table at the local Starbucks and started getting acquainted. Early in the conversation, after a bit of small talk, David wanted to be upfront with Lonnie about our financial situation, so he decided to pull the Band-aid off fast. He said in the kindest way he could, "Listen, before we get started, I want to be upfront with you. We're not looking to hire anyone right now, so I don't want to waste your time or give the wrong impression. We're actually trying to build a building right now."

Immediately, something changed in the air. Lonnie seemed to be leaning into the conversation with a heightened interest, and began asking more questions about our church's story and our own leadership journey. David shared that we had been trying for years to build a building on our property, but we had never been able to get the project off the ground. He recounted all of the false starts, dead ends, and lessons learned the hard way. The more they talked,

David started to get the strange sense that God might, in fact, be "up to something" through this meeting.

When it was finally Lonnie's turn to share, he got right to point: "Well, now I know why God brought us together. In addition to being a pastor, myself, I'm also a church builder—and I think I can help you." David couldn't believe what he was hearing. They finished the conversation, agreeing to just keep in touch…and see where things might lead. But before Lonnie headed back toward home, he asked if he could see our property; so, the two of them got in their separate cars and made the 10-minute drive to Hutto.

A WATER TOWER MIRACLE

As they pulled onto the property, they parked at the base of a large water tower. Much to David's surprise, when Lonnie got out of his truck, he had tears in his eyes once again. (*Honestly, at that point, David was probably thinking, "What is with this guy? He sure cries a lot!"*)

But then Lonnie shared something incredible. In fact, his story was downright CRAZY. He explained that two and a half years earlier, he and his wife, Debbie, were driving to San Antonio from their home near Fort Worth. Their plan was to spend a fun weekend getting away with some friends. They had heard about a new toll road that had opened, which would allow drivers to bypass Austin traffic altogether—so they decided to check it out. As they drove, a certain water tower just happened to catch Lonnie's attention. It had the name "Manville" painted on the side. Instantly, Lonnie heard the Lord say, "I want you to build a church in Manville." He didn't know exactly what that meant, but He knew God had spoken.

Days later, when he got back home, he started searching for demographics and other information about the city of Manville. He wanted to learn everything he could about this community, but he came up empty. What Lonnie didn't know (but Austin residents would understand) is that Manville wasn't a city, at all. It was just the name of the water company that services that community. The actual town was Hutto.

So Lonnie eventually just let it go. He second-guessed himself. Maybe it wasn't God speaking to him after all. Maybe he just missed it.

Yet, now here he was, standing under that very same water tower two and a half years later, talking to David about building a church there! Isn't that CRAZY?

Remember...God is in the crazy.

From that day forward, things started falling into place. We trusted Lonnie to lead the construction project, even though his process was a little unconventional, to say the least! He promised to take our plans for an 18,500 sqft building—(the projected cost of which was $3.2 million)—and build it for our modest budget of $1.2 million. (Yes, you read that correctly. It was a $2 million savings!)

At first, it sounded too good to be true. But then we realized how he planned to accomplish this amazing feat. As you may recall, Lonnie was a pastor of his own church— but knowing his heart for the Kingdom, his elder board agreed to let him divide his time between Fort Worth and Hutto. The plan was for him to build our church while continuing to pastor his own. *(Crazy right?)* In real time, would mean countless hours on the road, and juggling responsibilities in two places. Without God, it would have seemed impossible. But Lonnie is just wired different. His radical faith is matched only by his radical work ethic. I honestly believe that while Lonnie was working all that "overtime" on our building, the enemy was also working overtime to take him out. In fact, Lonnie even overcame a cancer diagnosis and extensive surgery during the time he was working on our project. So after only 15 months full of long hours and hands-on work, the building was finally finished—on schedule and under budget—all for $1.2 million.

It was nothing short of a miracle.

God is in the crazy.

LITTLE BY LITTLE...UNTIL

That one obedient step—saying yes to a random golf tournament invite—opened a door we didn't know existed.

Faith doesn't always feel big. Sometimes it feels like coffee with a stranger. Sometimes it feels like one more "yes" after hundreds of disappointments.

That's what leadership in the wilderness requires. Not massive leaps. Just consistent, faithful steps—even when you're tired. Even when you feel alone. Because legacy isn't built in grand gestures. It's built in perseverance. **So stick with it!**

We used to think progress meant momentum—open doors, fast movement, clear timelines. But what we actually experienced was something far less glamorous, but more formational. Steady, painful obedience over time.

That was our reality for seven years. (*7 years that felt like 40.*)

Like the Israelites wandering around in the desert, we were wandering, too. Circling the same questions, the same delays, the same stretch of dry, dusty hope.

No building. No movement. Just waiting.

Wilderness experiences can be hard to endure—but even harder to understand. We find ourselves asking, "Where is God in all of this? Why is this happening?"

UNDERSTANDING THE TENSION IN THE TIMING

When it comes to better understanding **the tension of God's timing**, there is no one-size-fits-all explanation—but we can learn from the examples found in Scripture. Consider the way God dealt with His own people, the Israelites. At times, He was *punishing* them for disobedience. Other times, He was *preparing* them for something ahead.

Sometimes the waiting is *punishment.*

In Numbers 14, we read that God became angry with His people because they did not place their trust in Him. After the twelve spies had spent forty days secretly exploring the land of Canaan, ten of them came back with a negative report, spreading fear among the people. Only Joshua and Caleb had faith that God would grant them success—but their opinion was overruled, so the people grumbled against Moses. God's reaction was swift and strong. He condemned them to wander for 40 years—one year for each day of their exploration—until all their bodies fell in the wilderness. Only Joshua and Caleb—and their families—would survive to see the Promised Land.

Sometimes the waiting is *preparation.*

In this context, God is giving instructions through his servant Moses for His chosen people to live by as they prepare to inhabit the Promised Land. After commanding them to obeying the law, observe the Sabbath, and recognize the annual festivals, beginning in verse 20, He turns His attention toward their future. God promises to send an angel ahead of them to guard them along the way and to bring them to the place He has prepared. He promises to bless them with health, fertility, and long lives. *(Sounds pretty great so far, huh?)* Next, He promises to go before them, sending terror and confusion upon their enemies, causing them to turn their backs and run. And if that doesn't work, He'll even send hornets to drive out anyone who is left.

The Israelites must have been thinking, "How awesome is this?!? Sounds like God is giving us a green light. Pedal to the metal. Let's go!!" (At least that's what I would be saying.)

But then in verse 29, God taps the brakes:

> "I will not drive them out in a single year, because the land would become desolate and the wild animals too numerous for you. Little by little I will drive them out before you, until you have increased enough to take possession of the land." (Exodus 23:29)

Here was the problem: **They were NOT READY to inhabit this new land.**

There were other nations presently occupying that land. They had huge armies with horses and chariots. And even if God helped the Israelites defeat those armies—and cleared the path ahead of them—they weren't actually ready to live there.

This is so practical! God is simply saying, "YOU'RE NOT READY…so we're gonna take this slow. I'm still developing you. I'm still watching you. I'm still STRETCHING you.

> "30 **Little by little** I will drive them out before you, **until** you have increased enough to take possession of the land." (Exodus 23:29-30)

Little by little…until.

Can I just encourage you today: Be OK with God's pace. Be OK with God's process.

Be OK with these words: "LITTLE BY LITTLE" (I know that doesn't sound very exciting. We want it all NOW…if not yesterday!).

But notice the next word: "UNTIL"

> ...you have increased enough

> ...you have grown enough

> ...your character has developed

> ...the "INSIDE" change can be seen on the outside

> ...the PRIVATE life is something I can promote publicly

Little. By. Little.

Here is the principle:

The PACE of your GROWTH is determined by God's assessment of your POTENTIAL.

The pace of God's process is always intentional. No short cuts. No quick wins. No "overnight sensations." No "one hit wonders." No promotions given that can't be sustained. He doesn't allow "premature promotion" in His Kingdom! In other words, God knows what He's doing.

> Whether a nation (in this case, Israel)

> Or a church...

> Or a ministry...

> Or a leader...

> Or any child of God

God doesn't send the VICTORY, the RESULTS, the BLESSING, the HARVEST...UNTIL YOU'RE READY!

Michele and I clung to that promise. It's not that God couldn't have handed over the full promise in a moment. It's that we couldn't have handled it. He wasn't just preparing the land—He was preparing *us*. And preparation takes time.

"Little by little until..."

Instead of asking, "*God, when will this end?*" we began asking, "*God, what are You preparing in us right now?*"

Instead of "*Why is this taking so long?*" we began asking, "*What do I need to learn while I wait?*"

If there's one thing we've learned: **The waiting is worth it.**

Why? Because at the end of the day, our hearts beat for one thing: **One more person finding Jesus. One more life transformed by the gospel**. And if we have to walk slowly, suffer deeply, or press forward little by little—*we'll do it.*

Because it's not about our comfort. It's about His kingdom. **More of Him. Less of us.**

Lastly, for those trying to make sense out of your own waiting and wandering, it's natural to ask the same question: Is this punishment, or preparation?

Only God knows his purpose for your waiting—(and He's not telling)—but His ways are always right. So, when you're going through your "wilderness," all you can really do is trust, obey, and keep taking steps.

If you're weary in the wait—hear this: **Stick with it.**

God is in this crazy. Keep going! He is with you—and He's preparing you for something greater than you can see right now.

Little by little... ***until.***

PRACTICAL TAKEAWAYS

» **Be interruptible.** Often, our plans are so detailed and driven that we leave no room for God to insert something unexpected. Divine appointments rarely show up in our calendar apps.

» **Pay attention to "coincidences."** The people you meet, the stories you hear, even the tears someone sheds—these may be spiritual signals, not emotional noise.

» **Discern, don't dismiss.** Not everyone who enters your life is sent by God, but some *absolutely* are. Don't dismiss something just because it's unconventional. Test it. Pray through it. Invite wise voices in.

» **Trust God's economics.** What looks too expensive, too impossible, or too unlikely may be exactly what God will use to show His glory.

» **Stick with the vision, even when others don't.** When you're walking in obedience, you won't always have majority approval. That's okay. Obedience is your responsibility. The outcome is God's.

REFLECTION QUESTIONS

Use these for personal reflection, couple conversations, or your leadership circle.

1. **Where might God be using divine interruption in my life right now to draw me into deeper trust?**

2. **What "crazy" thing in my current season might actually be God showing up?**

3. **When have I seen God work most powerfully through the unexpected or unconventional? What did I learn?**

STRETCH YOURSELF

"FAITH NEVER KNOWS
WHERE IT IS BEING LED, BUT
IT LOVES AND KNOWS THE
ONE WHO IS LEADING."
(OSWALD CHAMBERS)

"GOD IS MORE INTERESTED
IN YOUR CHARACTER
THAN YOUR COMFORT.
HE WILL STRETCH YOU TO
GROW YOUR FAITH."
(RICK WARREN)

CHAPTER 3:
(DAVID:)

As Michele and I have been writing this book together, it has been overwhelming to look back over the past 31 years of marriage and ministry, and to see the faithfulness of the God we serve. Of course, this is *His* story, not ours. This is *His* church, not ours. That's why our daily prayer has been, and will continue to be: **MORE of Him, LESS of us.**

Still yet, we are mindful of the fact that the cumulative effect of those experiences has changed us (hopefully for the better). We have grown. We have matured. We are different. Yes, we still have a long way to go—(we know that better than anyone)—but there is no denying the *change* that has taken place *in us* along this journey.

In a word, God has STRETCHED us. And not only us, but the church family we have been honored to lead. By the way, this is not unique to us, so please don't misunderstand my premise. No one can live as a disciple of Jesus Christ and stay the same. *No one.*

In fact, please let me say it another way:

FOLLOWING GOD WILL NEVER STOP REQUIRING FAITH.

We walk by FAITH, not by sight. Following God is a faith-filled journey…so get used to it! There's no other way to follow God except by faith. You will never "outgrow" the need for faith—it's just how we must live as disciples of Jesus.

Let's go one step further: If the way you're living right now is NOT requiring faith, then God's not happy. *(Ouch. That hurts...but it's true)*

> *And it is impossible to please God without faith. Anyone who wants to come to him must believe that God exists and that he rewards those who sincerely seek him. (Hebrews 11:6 NLT)*

There is no denying this truth. Faith is a requirement for faithfulness. So, if you want to one day hear the words of your Savior, "Well done, good and faithful servant," you'd better get comfortable with being uncomfortable. Let God stretch you.

There is a Scripture passage in **Isaiah 54:2-3** which provides a great picture of how we must allow God to stretch us.

> *2 "Enlarge the place of your tent, stretch your tent curtains wide, do not hold back; lengthen your cords, strengthen your stakes. 3 For you will spread out to the right and to the left; your descendants will dispossess nations and settle in their desolate cities." (Isaiah 54:2-3)*

To better understand this image, it is helpful to know that during Bible times, the Israelites ("God's people") lived a largely nomadic lifestyle. This started when they were delivered from slavery in Egypt by Moses (Exodus 12). Unfortunately, because of their lack of faith, they were afraid to invade the land of Canaan. This caused God to punish them by sending them into the wilderness, to wander around for 40 years. (By the way, during this time he still fed them, protected them, and guided them by His visible Presence—but nonetheless, He was definitely "teaching them a lesson!")

So, not only during their time in the wilderness, but even after they had entered into the "Promised Land" God had given them, the people were mobile. For generations, they traveled from place to place, fighting battles, conquering cities, and expanding the territory of God's people. During this time, they lived in **tents**. Not only did the people themselves live in tents, but even "God's house" was a tent – it was a "portable church" called a "tabernacle."

If you have ever been on a camping trip, you know the basic process of all tents is the same: Find a level spot, set up poles, cover them with some kind of canvas. Then, extend the ropes out to provide stability. Lastly, drive stakes into the ground to hold everything down.

Again, all tents basically follow this same assembly process. For small tents, it's pretty easy. But the bigger the tent, the more challenging the process. Why? Because you will probably be dealing with taller poles, wider curtains, longer ropes, and stronger stakes.

Then if you make the jump from a family-size tent to a venue-size tent (like the kind often utilized for wedding receptions or outdoor concerts), you would expect the set-up time to be much longer. Now just imagine how big of an undertaking it must be to erect a large circus tent! We're talking hundreds of pieces, a large crew of workers, and probably some heavy machinery. It would be an all day process. Why so long? The answer is obvious.

The bigger the tent, the more preparation is needed!

To fit more people underneath, you'll need a larger tent. To secure the tent in heavy winds, you'll need to make sure it is anchored down properly. Because if the tent isn't secure, the people won't be safe! So, everything always comes back to these same basic requirements:

Taller poles. Wider curtains. Longer ropes. Stronger stakes.

In this chapter, we want to share some of the lessons we have learned—both personally and as a church—by allowing God to stretch us. But as you keep reading, ask yourself the question: *Am I allowing God to stretch me?*

Remember, you always have a choice: stretch, or play it safe?

1.   WHEREVER YOU ARE ON YOUR JOURNEY OF FAITH, THERE'S MORE.

"Enlarge the place of your tent..." (Isaiah 54:2)

When we moved into our new building on Sunday June 1, 2014, it felt like we had finally crossed the finish line of a long, hard race. God had truly done a miracle! With the help of our friend, Lonnie Huett, we had completed the construction project—and, after seven years in our "portable church wilderness," our church finally had a home of our own again.

It's hard to describe how Michele and I felt on that first Sunday. There were so many emotions running through us all at once. On the one hand, I felt a sense of relief. Knowing the long journey we had taken to get to that moment, part of me was just glad it was over! The last year had been filled with challenges, prayers, and sacrifices, and standing there in a space we had dreamed of for so long made it all feel real. At the same time, I felt a little proud (in a good way, if that's even possible) because this was our first time building a church from the ground up—and we had done it! It hadn't been easy; some people from our congregation had left along the way, which made the moment even more meaningful. To see it completed, to gather and worship in that space, was a deeply emotional and unforgettable experience.

STRETCHING IN TIMES OF LOSS

But just four days later, our world was shaken. Todd Davis, our associate pastor and dear friend of over twenty years, was killed in a tragic car accident. Todd, along with his wife Cindy, had worked tirelessly day and night to prepare the building as we came down the homestretch. This was the kind of news nothing could ever prepare you for—and it was the last thing we expected during a week meant for celebration. Michele and I were devastated, as was our entire congregation, and of course, no one more so than Cindy.

In the immediate aftermath of this tragedy, I did my best to fulfil my "pastoral role," even though I was still in shock myself. After all, I *was* the pastor. Michele and I spent the next couple of days in Dallas, doing whatever we could to comfort Cindy and the rest of the family. Of course, funeral preparations needed to be handled. Todd had died on a Thursday, and since the funeral wouldn't be until Monday, I left for home on Saturday night in order to be at church on Sunday.

The 3-hour drive home that night gave me some much-needed time to think and pray. I had never experienced a loss like that, and the timing left me reeling. Just days after the highest pinnacle of our ministry lives, we were struggling to make sense of it all. I just couldn't believe Todd was gone. The very person who had poured his life into preparing our new spiritual home would never get to serve in it. This was not how things were supposed to go.

When I walked into church the next morning, I felt completely inadequate for the task. But a friend of mine had given me some godly wisdom the night before, and I intended to use it. Our plan was to open the service with a couple of worship choruses, and then I would share the news with the church family, giving whatever details I could share. Some of the people who came that morning knew nothing about it. Keep in mind, this was only the second week our new building was open.

After speaking for no more than fifteen minutes, I opened the floor to anyone who wanted to speak. Some asked questions. Others shared memories of Todd. Many offered words of condolences to Cindy, her family. Still others recited Scripture verses. We even had a few first-time visitors in the house that day, and a couple of them spoke as well. (Can you imagine walking into a church for the first time and experiencing an atmosphere like that? I know of at least one family who visited that day and is still part of our church eleven years later! They later told me that if a church responded that way during times of grieving, they knew it was a place they could call home.)

That experience was indescribably painful, but it **stretched** us. One Sunday we celebrated. The next Sunday we mourned. Our initial introduction into the community was one marked with both heart-breaking vulnerability and heart-lifting joy. In His own personal and powerful way, God reminded us that He is the One who brings beauty from ashes, joy for mourning, the garment of praise for the heavy in spirit (Isaiah 61:3).

We couldn't see it at the time, but I believe God was using that tragedy—and more importantly, our response to it—to shape the culture of our church family for generations to come. To deepen our love for one another. He was re-deeming the loss. He was working all things together for good. He was stretching us. **Enlarging our tent**...so that countless others who are hurting and broken could come "home" and find their Father waiting.

GROWTH ONLY COMES THROUGH STRETCHING

In the months that followed, God continued to move in our midst. Our weekly attendance quickly grew from the 100 people who came with us to 250 and beyond. By October 2014, only four months removed from the grand opening, we were ready to launch a second service! (This is a common practice in many churches today, but for us it was unprecedented.) We learned the hard way that a second service isn't as simple as just duplicating everything we just did an hour earlier. You can't just "hit the repeat button." There's a lot of planning, recruiting, training, and mobilizing involved. We're talking twice the greeters, twice the ushers, twice the nursery workers. It also means twice the donuts, twice the diapers, and twice the coffee cups. Not to mention, the worship team stays twice as long. The pastor preaches twice as long (well, hopefully not!). Everything would be different...and we had some catching up to do!

Here's something I have noticed: the vision God places in our hearts will almost always be one (or two...or three) steps ahead of what we think we can handle. He doesn't wait for us to feel ready. Ready or not, He promises to help us. We knew God was **enlarging** our tent and expanding our vision. Our emotions, our resources, and our team were definitely being **stretched**. It wasn't going to be easy—but it would be worth it!

2. THE PROVISION IS IN THE STRETCHING

(MICHELE:)

"...stretch your tent curtains wide, do not hold back..."
(Isaiah 54:2)

VISION WILL ALWAYS OUTPACE RESOURCES

We have a message for any leader reading this: It's normal to feel scared or hesitant when taking big steps of faith—especially when finances are involved.

WE DARE YOU TO BELIEVE IN A GOD OF ABUNDANCE, NOT SCARCITY

Again, it's *normal*. We've been there. Yes, we know bills, budgets and business meetings can be scary. However, we dare you to believe in a God of abundance, not scarcity.

May we never forget, this isn't our church—it's His. We are just stewards. And because it's His church, He will take responsibility for providing whatever is needed to accomplish His purposes.

Your vision will always feel too big—so God must stretch your faith to match it.

Often times God's stretching can be scary, but sometimes it can be a blast! Not sure about that? Are you a little skeptical that serving God can actually be fun? Well, just keep reading. This next story is for you...

In the spring of 2015, I spent the weekend visiting a friend in Colorado. Since David and I are pastors, we rarely have the opportunity to visit other churches (because we are at our own, obviously)—so I was excited to attend hers on that Sunday morning. The name of the church was Flatirons, a large multi-site church with locations all around the Denver metropolitan area.

The morning I visited just so happened to be the same weekend as their special needs prom event called, "SHINE." The only reason I know this is because they took time during the service to play a recap video of the event. It was amazing! Tears streamed down my face as I watched the sheer joy of these amazing people, dancing the night away, seemingly without a care in the world. I was captivated. The video couldn't have lasted longer than 3 minutes, but the images I saw left an immediate and lasting impact. Their celebration became my call to action.

I knew in that very moment we *had* to do this in our community.

When I got back to Austin after the weekend, the first thing I did was show David the video from Flatirons Church. He responded the same way I did—tears and all. We tossed around a few ideas of the best way to share this idea with our church, but in the end, we simply decided to show the video. So that's exactly what we did. We showed *their* video in *our* church the following Sunday. *(What a crazy idea, huh?)*

Needless to say, that 3-minute video was all it took to capture the hearts of our church family. That next Monday night we held an interest meeting, and over 30 people came! Now we just had to put our heads together and figure out how to pull it off...in only six weeks. We had no money, no decorations, no theme, no plan, no volunteers, and perhaps most importantly...no one to attend, yet!

But one way or another, *it was going to happen.* **Vision always outpaces resources**. No money? No problem. If God puts something in your heart to accomplish, you can trust that He's willing and able to pay for it.

Six weeks later, by the grace of God, we rolled out the red carpet *(literally, not figuratively)* for our first-ever "SHINE" prom for individuals with special needs. Our guests were treated to an extravagant night of limousine rides, delicious food, event t-shirts, giveaways, pictures with their favorite super heroes, and of course dancing—*lots* of dancing.

Oh and by the way, at the time of this writing, we will have just recently celebrated our 10th annual SHINE prom! Won't He do it!

GET READY FOR GREATER

In the fall of 2017, our leadership team began to have some preliminary discussion about an upcoming milestone in our church's history: the 80th anniversary of Bridge Church (formerly Central Assembly of God). Opportunities like this don't exactly come around very often, so we wanted to host a celebration worthy of such a special occasion. One of the first questions posed to me regarding the event came from the decorating team. *(Everyone knows how CRAZY those church party planners can be, right?)* They were asking for the *theme* of the upcoming celebration. I have to admit, I was initially caught off guard by how important this seemed to them. After all, I thought "80th Anniversary Celebration" was a perfectly good theme. *(Apparently not.)*

So I asked for a few weeks to think (and pray) about it, but promised to get back to them. Settling on a theme was actually harder than I expected. Our goal was two-fold. First, we definitely wanted to honor the spiritual heritage of those who had gone before us, the shoulders upon which we stand. But secondly, of course, this was a perfect opportunity to share a compelling, faith-filled vision for our future—one that would last another eight decades, if the Lord is willing!

Once I got quiet before the Lord, it didn't take long for Him to direct my heart to one particular passage of Scripture:

> 6 *"This is what the Lord Almighty says: 'In a little while I will once more shake the heavens and the earth, the sea and the dry land. 7 I will shake all nations, and what is desired by all nations will come, and I will fill this house with glory,' says the Lord Almighty. 8 'The silver is mine and the gold is mine,' declares the Lord Almighty. 9* ***'The glory of this present house will be greater than the glory of the former house,'*** *says the Lord Almighty. 'And in this place I will grant peace,' declares the Lord Almighty."* (Haggai 2:6-9)

The more time I spent meditating on the promises found within this passage, the more excited my heart became. God is boldly declaring that GREATER things are coming. Greater glory is coming. Greater resources are coming. Greater anointing is coming.

As you may already guessed, "GREATER" became the theme for our celebration. But this wasn't just a nice idea for the decoration team to run with—it suddenly felt like much more than that. We sensed it was a prophetic word over Bridge Church. God was preparing us for greater influence, greater impact, and yes, greater responsibility. He was **stretching** us to believe for GREATER.

(NOTE: By the way, in chapter 6 of this book, we will explore more fully some of the principles found in Haggai 2:6-9 and share the profound impact this revelation has had on our church family.)

OBEDIENCE IS WHAT FAITH LOOKS LIKE

One of the most significant ways we have pursued this "GREATER" vision is in the area of our finances. For many years, our church had struggled financially. Budgets were tight. Reserves were nonexistent. Income was low. Stress was high. You've heard the term "living paycheck to paycheck" – well, as a church, we were living "Sunday offering to Sunday offering."

Something needed to change.

So, in 2018, we committed that 10% of every dollar received would go directly to missions—no conditions, no delay. Our logic was simple: If tithing works for the individual believer, why aren't we practicing it as a church? The truth is we had always wanted to become more generous in the area of missions giving, but I am ashamed to say it was fear that held us back.

We called it the Kingdom Builders Fund. Through it, we are committed to making a difference around the block and around the world. We started funding local outreach, church planting, global missions, and more. It wasn't comfortable. But it was obedient. And God honored it. That year alone, our team went on four different mission trips—more than ever before. As we stretched, God multiplied. Finances grew, our reach expanded, and our people were trans-formed.

Every year since then, the fund has grown. Each year, we've said YES to more opportunities to spread the Gospel. Why? Because God can trust us. If we teach tithing to indi-viduals, we must model it as a church. Not just to appear generous—but because *obedience is what faith looks like.* Saying YES to Kingdom Builders has been one of the most defining decisions in our financial journey—and one of the clearest ways we've seen God's faithfulness at work.

3. THE POTENTIAL IS IN THE STRETCHING

"Lengthen your cords..." — Isaiah 54:2

Before continuing our story, let's begin with a quick discus-sion of the word *potential.* By definition it means, "having latent qualities or abilities that may be developed and lead to future success or usefulness." It probably seems strange to look up a definition *within* a definition, but to fully appre-ciate the meaning of this chapter, let's make sure you under-stand the meaning of the word *latent*, too. By definition, latent means, "(of a quality or state of) existing but not yet developed or manifest; hidden or concealed."

In other words, if something has **potential,** that means it has *hidden* or *concealed* qualities—(*latent* qualities)—*already existing, but not yet developed.* Once developed, however, these qualities will lead to future success or usefulness.

To put it a different way, when something or someone has *potential*, there is **more inside of them** than what can be seen at first glance. Hidden or concealed qualities. Some-thing not yet developed. There is potential that just hasn't been realized...YET. And this is EXACTLY the kind of people whom God wants to use to accomplish His work...and ulti-mately, to demonstrate His glory.

WHAT DOES GOD SEE?

Perhaps you've heard it said this way: **God is not looking for ABILITY; He's looking for AVAILABILITY.** If you and I are willing to personally apply this statement to our own lives, it raises lots of questions for further reflection: *Am I willing to be used? Am I willing to be stretched? Am I willing to be available for whatever potential usefulness which God sees in me but that I don't even see in myself?*

In his first letter to the Corinthian church, Paul's purpose for writing is to bring instruction and correction—which he probably knows will be difficult for them to hear. But notice how he doesn't start off by saying, *"Hey everyone, you better listen to me because I'm in charge! I'm your leader! I'm kind of a big deal...so pay attention!"*

In fact, he pretty much says the opposite. Listen to his humility—as he makes it clear, **"This is NOT about me."**

> *When I came to you, I did not come with **eloquence** or **human wisdom** as I proclaimed to you the testimony about God. 2 For I resolved to know nothing while I was with you except Jesus Christ and him crucified. 3 I came to you in **weakness** with **great fear and trembling**. 4 My message and my preaching were not with wise and persuasive words, but with a demonstration of the Spirit's power, 5 so that your faith might not rest on human wisdom, but on God's power. (1 Corinthians 2:1-5)*

See how he is modeling the principle: **"More of Him, less of me"**

Then, notice how he turns the attention from HIMSELF...to THEM:

> *26 Brothers and sisters, **think of what YOU were when you were called**. Not many of you were **wise** by human standards; not many were **influential**; not many were **of noble birth**. (1 Corinthians 1:26)*

He's pointing out they weren't much in man's eyes, but God chose to use them anyway! He's telling them God doesn't just use <u>WISE</u> people, or <u>STRONG</u> people, or <u>INFLUENTIAL</u> people. Keep reading…

> *27 But God chose the **foolish** things of the world to shame the wise; God chose the **weak** things of the world to shame the strong. 28 God chose the **lowly** things of this world and the **despised** things—and the things that are not—to nullify the things that are, 29 so that no one may boast before him. 30 It is because of him that you are in Christ Jesus, who has become for us wisdom from God—that is, our righteousness, holiness and redemption. 31 Therefore, as it is written: "Let the one who boasts boast in the Lord." (1 Corinthians 2:27-31)*

God chooses foolish… instead of wise.

Weak… instead of strong.

Nobodies… instead of somebodies.

Washed-up people past their prime… instead of the best-and-brightest!

He chooses people who are too young, too old, too broken, too damaged. (*…all the people we probably wouldn't use, if we were in charge.*)

THERE IS MORE IN YOU THAT GOD WANTS TO USE

The main point here is that **God chooses people the world doesn't see any potential in.**

He sees their "latent qualities" (those things that are hidden or concealed). He knows perfectly how to develop them… because He created them. He sees what future success they are capable of…because He already knows the future.

So, here's the million-dollar question: **How exactly does God bring out all of this potential He sees?**

The answer is simple: He stretches it… then releases it to fly!

To illustrate this principle, just pick up an ordinary **rubber band**. *(If you're like me, you can probably find one in the junk drawer at your kitchen counter. So if you want to run grab one for this little object lesson, we'll wait…)*

You know how this works, but let's do it together anyway. Go ahead, pull back the rubber band. The more you pull it back, the further it stretches. When you release the pressure, it will return to its original shape. Like nothing ever happened. No harm, no foul. No adventure. Nothing to see here.

HE CHOOSES PEOPLE WHO ARE TOO YOUNG, TOO OLD, TOO BROKEN, TOO DAMAGED

But if, on the other hand, you actually wanted to send the rubber band flying across the room, you would have to stretch it back…**and release it.** Naturally, the further you stretch the rubber band, the more *resistance* you begin to feel. If it could talk, the rubber band would probably tell you it doesn't like the stretching. It's uncomfortable. But in this *tension* is where the *potential* lives.

Don't miss this.

The rubber band was *made* to be stretched. That is the very *purpose* for its existence.

The same is true for you. You were *made* to be stretched. In that tension is where your *potential* lives. So are you willing to allow God to stretch you…and then release you to fly?

PURPOSE IN THE PAIN

(MICHELE:)

2017 was a very difficult year for me, personally.

During that one year, I walked through the painful loss of several close family members, one after another. David's uncle passed away on New Year's Day. In May, I lost my dad after a short battle with respiratory illness, due to lung damage he received during his service in Vietnam. Then in December, my brother died very unexpectedly, followed by another beloved uncle who had been a lifelong mentor and my basketball coach. It felt like David and I were going from heartbreak to heartbreak, funeral to funeral. At times the grief and loss seemed to overwhelm me, and I found myself seeking God more deeply than ever.

One of the beautiful byproducts of a relationship with God is that His strength shows up in our weakness. He draws near to the brokenhearted. He walks with us through the dark valleys. He carries us when we don't think we can go another step. Even though David and I preach this stuff all the time, *everything* I believed about the love of my heavenly Father became more *real* that year. He comforted me in a way no one else could. For that, I am forever grateful.

But something else happened that I didn't expect. In my pain, **God's voice became clearer.**

Throughout my life, I have learned that **while the world is shouting, God whispers.** This was never more true than during my "Year of Funerals." Like Elijah, the discouraged prophet, I stood at the dark door of my own hiding place, wondering where God was in all of this. Wondering what the future had in store. Wondering what I should do next. Wondering if I would ever feel like myself again. I was exhausted, and I just needed God to show up one more time. That's exactly what happened.

But God's presence didn't show up in a mighty wind, or an earthquake, or fire.

He came in a gentle whisper. And this is what I heard him say:

> *"I'm going to be asking you to do some uncomfortable things. They will be new and different. You won't understand, but I want you to be ready to* **SAY YES."**

GET READY FOR YOUR YES

So I prepared my heart to obey. Whenever God spoke, my answer would be YES. In fact, funny story. I was so deeply moved during this whole season that I actually decided to get my first tattoo. *(By the way, at the time of this writing, it is still my only tattoo, but we'll see how long that lasts! I've got some ideas for #2...)* The tattoo simply says, **YES.** Whenever people ask about it, I tell them the *period* is intentional. In other words, the exact meaning is "YES *period*."

God doesn't want my answer to be, "YES, but I'll think about it." Or "YES, but I'm not quite ready yet." Or "YES, but are you sure this isn't a job for someone else?"

He wants my answer (and yours) to be, **"YES *period*!"**

It wasn't long before I began to recognize the shift was already happening. In the spring of 2018, I was invited by a friend, Sandie Mundis, to accompany her on a missions trip in Vienna, Austria. Sandie and her husband, Greg, had served as career missionaries with the Assemblies of God, and at that time, Greg was serving as the Executive Director of world missions. To say we were humbled by the invitation would be a massive understatement. David and I were excited about the opportunity to visit Europe, but due to scheduling concerns and financial limitations, we were hesitant to pull the trigger on going. In fact, Sandie kept following up, but each time I just told her we'd think about it.

But Sandie wouldn't leave us alone, and neither would God. He kept nudging my heart, reminding me of my promise to Him. This was my chance to take a step of obedience. So finally, we said yes. That single yes would change so much more than we expected.

The purpose of the trip was to join Sandie in attending the first-ever Christian women's conference in a public venue in Austria. This would be a historic moment. "Inspire Vienna," as it was called, was being sponsored through the ministry of Vienna Christian Center (VCC), led by pastors Larry and Melinda Henderson. VCC is an international church with a vision to make Jesus known throughout the world, so this women's conference was born out of that DNA. Over 1,000 women from fifty different nations attended. We witnessed healings, salvations, and saw 63 women receive their very first Bibles. It was an amazing few days!

During one of the altar moments, I walked to the front of the room so that I could be available to serve as part of prayer team. While I was ministering to some of the ladies who had responded, something happened that caught me by surprise.

God whispered.

*It wasn't an audible voice, but in that moment, I **knew** He was speaking to my heart. Just as clearly as you're reading the words on this page right now, I "heard" God say:*

"I want you to do something like this back home."

I wish I could tell you that I answered, "YES period!" But that wouldn't be true. Instead, I jumped straight to negotiation mode: "Lord, in case you didn't know, I live in the United States and there at lots of opportunities like this back home. In fact, on any given weekend, there are probably 2 or 3 different women's conferences within driving distance from my house. How about if I just load up the church van and take a bunch of ladies to one of them? You don't need me to do this. Austin has enough conferences already!"

His next response was even clearer: *"This will be different. Will you trust me to lead you?"*

I still didn't know what to say. I needed time to process what I was hearing and feeling. But as I walked back to my seat, one of our team members met me in the aisle. She looked directly into my eyes and said, "Pastor Michele, God wants you to do a conference like this in Austin."

That moment confirmed the calling. The conversation was over. I was ready to give God my YES *period*. And from that one act of obedience, our "SHE IS" conference was born. God has completely transformed the women and girls of our Bridge Church family. That yes led to a fresh move of God among the women in our church. Leadership emerged. Faith deepened. Callings answered. What started as a whisper became a movement. A beautiful Sisterhood.

4.   THE MIRACLE IS IN THE STRETCHING

 US:

"Strengthen your stakes…" — Isaiah 54:2

There are countless stories in the Bible of God calling people out of their comfort zones. And with each one, the stretching brought miraculous blessings they'd never imagined.

> »   Abraham trusted God for the child he was promised, even despite his and his wife's advanced age. His faith-***stretching*** ended with a little baby in his arms named Isaac, who was a fulfillment of God's covenant promise. (Genesis 21:1-7)

» Jesus' disciples feared for their lives when a violent storm threatened to sink their boat. But Peter's faith was **stretched** when he stepped out of the boat at Jesus' invitation, and he miraculously walked on water. (Matthew 14:22-33)

» Jesus told a crippled man, with muscles weak and atrophied, to get up and walk. The man stretched his faith as he **stretched** out his legs and walked for the very first time. (Matthew 9:1-7)

» Joshua must have felt ridiculous leading the Israelites to circle the walls of Jericho seven times, but his faith was **stretched**—as were the people he led—and eventually the walls came crumbling down. (Joshua 6)

God calls us all to do some faith stretching now and then. Whether we are called to leave our comfort zones to obey and act, or to rest and trust God during a difficult season of life, He always rewards great faith with wonderful blessings.

As our church was continuing to grow, we found ourselves outgrowing our building faster than we had imagined. It was both thrilling and terrifying. The miracle construction project we had accomplished only 5 years earlier, with the help of God (and Lonnie), had served its purpose well—but we had outgrown it. From one service to two, and eventually three—we no longer had enough space to contain the people God was sending. It was time to talk about building again.

GOD'S PLANS ARE BETTER

We quickly developed a strategy to construct a brand new auditorium and nursery area, which would allow us to repurpose our existing multipurpose building for youth and kids ministries. Then we would connect the parking lots to give everything a multi-building "campus" feel. Done. Easy-peasy. Let's do it.

We had the plans drawn up and were only months away from breaking ground when we heard some unsettling rumors about a Williamson County road project that might possibly be coming through our neck of the woods. At first, we dismissed the rumors as hearsay. But they didn't go away. If what we were hearing was true, the County was making plans to put this new road project directly through our property. Not just nearby—they were planning to cut it in half!

In time, those rumors were confirmed. We soon met with officials from the county, asking them to reconsider their placement of the road. The conversations were cordial, but in the end, unproductive. Their plans were already set in stone. So instead of protesting further, we turned our attention towards negotiating a fair sales price. As negotiations go, they gave a low-ball offer, we asked for the moon, and we settled somewhere in the middle.

But here is the miracle: The "somewhere in the middle" price was no less than $6.25 million dollars! We couldn't believe in the faithfulness of God.

MIRACLES FOLLOW THE STRETCHING

(MICHELE:)

Allow me to recap: Back in 2007, God had enabled us to buy an entire 73 acres—which, as you may recall, was in the middle of nowhere—for a modest $1.6 million. That land in Hutto then sat completely untouched for the next seven years while we wandered around in portable church "wilderness." (Not to mention, we were forced to spend over a quarter million dollars in taxes during those years to our good friends at Williamson County. Even though churches are supposed to be tax-exempt, since we still didn't have an "official" building on the property, we eventually lost our exemption.) In 2014, Lonnie Huett helped us construct a building valued at $3.2 million for only $1.2 million. That's quite a savings. That facility had served us well, but we had outgrown it. Now at the exact time we were making plans to build, God brokered a deal whereby we would receive $6.25 million (*from the government, mind you*) for our existing church building and 8 acres. What an awesome and faithful God we serve!

Every one of those **miracles** came in a time or season of **stretching**. And we were about to experience another one.

OBEDIENCE IS WHAT FAITH LOOKS LIKE.

In March of 2020, the entire world came screeching to a halt. A global pandemic named "COVID-19" changed everything—and Bridge Church was not exempt. Like so many churches across the country, we made the difficult decision to discontinue public gatherings. Something we thought would only last a week or two continued for over four months.

While the world was sheltering in place, we believed that eventually things would go back to normal—or at least whatever the *new normal* would be. And when that happened, we needed to be ready. And since the county bought our building (which we were leasing back), we had no choice but to build a new one.

A GOOD TIME FOR A GROUNDBREAKING

(DAVID:)

Looking back, I still remember how strange it felt to be meeting with architects, designing a building three times larger than the one we were leaving—during a time when no one was even going to church at all! This seemed ridiculous. But sure enough, on August 30, 2020, we officially broke ground on our new building!

Building a new facility during the chaos of COVID—when many churches were closing their doors—was not a popular decision. Even within our own church, some were not supportive. They warned us not to spend one dollar more than the $7 million we had on hand. Certainly, you can build a lot for that amount of money—but we didn't want to downsize the vision, solely based out of fear or scarcity. We knew God was leading us to build bigger, to stretch further, and to prepare for the growth we could've never seen coming.

This new building would not just serve our needs; it would become a launching pad. It would stretch us into a new level of ministry. It meant creating space for more families, more students, more kids, and more moments with God. And we weren't just building a place for people who were already there—we were building for the people who hadn't come yet.

To us, stretching didn't just mean growing numerically—it meant living with open hands and open hearts. It meant doing hard things when they didn't make sense. It meant giving away when it would've been safer to save. God would honor the stretch.

When all the designs were completed, and all the bids came back, the total budget for our new home was projected to be a whopping $10 million. Once again, at the time we signed those contracts, churches all over America were sitting completely empty—including ours. At best, it seemed risky. At worst, downright foolish. Who knows, some people probably thought the whole idea was CRAZY. But after all, **obedience is what faith looks like.**

It was putting our feet into the water. It was saying yes period. It was stretching...

Remember, God is (*always*) in the crazy.

PRACTICAL TAKEAWAYS

» **Stretching means walking in faith when finances don't make sense.**
God's vision always exceeds our resources—but He is always faithful.

» **Obedience may look crazy to others—but it positions you for God's best.**
Trust His timing and provision.

» **Your 'yes' unlocks new doors.**
When you step out, God meets you with affirmation and impact.

» **Endurance is not optional.**
God builds maturity, peace, and leadership character through the long, stretching seasons.

» **Multiplication comes after the stretch.**
When you make room—spiritually, financially, emotionally—God fills it beyond what you can ask or imagine.

REFLECTION QUESTIONS

Use these for personal reflection, couple conversations, or your leadership circle.

1. **Where is God asking me to stretch right now?**

2. **What am I afraid of losing if I say yes to God's next step?**

3. **How can I practically reinforce (strengthen my stakes) in this season?**

4. **Am I trusting God with my provision, or trying to manage outcomes myself?**

5. **Have I been resisting something that might actually be a divine invitation to grow?**

6. **What could God do through my life if I stopped playing it safe?**

"THE GREATEST SINGLE CAUSE OF ATHEISM IN THE WORLD TODAY IS CHRISTIANS WHO ACKNOWLEDGE JESUS WITH THEIR LIPS AND WALK OUT THE DOOR AND DENY HIM BY THEIR LIFESTYLE."
(BRENNAN MANNING, THE RAGAMUFFIN GOSPEL)

CHAPTER 4:
MICHELE:

Be real. Such a simple statement.

But it isn't just a nice idea to me—it's a deep conviction. As a Spirit-empowered woman, a mom raising four daughters, a business builder, and a co-pastor leading alongside my husband, I've seen firsthand the power of being fully, unapologetically who God created me to be. In a world constantly pressuring us to perform, to conform, to tone it down—I say no.

Be real. The world doesn't need more copies; it needs courageous originals.

That passion didn't come out of nowhere. It was planted in me years ago.

Growing up in church, if I'm honest, a lot of the pastors I saw didn't seem real. They weren't necessarily unkind or insincere—but they felt untouchable. They looked polished, talked polished, and seemed to live in a world I could never access. As a young girl watching from the pews, I started to believe that ministry was for a special type of person—the kind who had it all together and could perform behind a pulpit without a crack in their voice or a wrinkle in their story.

PASTORS ARE REAL PEOPLE.... WHO KNEW?

But at 12 years old, God used two very real, very down-to-earth pastors to flip that narrative. Their names were Charletta and Otis Garrison. When they were voted in by the small, rural congregation at First Assembly of God in Beggs, Oklahoma, there was no way of knowing what an impact their family would have on the course of my life.

They were normal in the best way. Their leadership wasn't just from the stage; it was from the kitchen table. They didn't try to be perfect—but they were present. They saw me. They listened. They laughed. They prayed. I watched them—not from a distance, but up close and personal, and through their authenticity, they made me believe that maybe—just maybe—one day God could use someone like me.

Otis wasn't the kind of pastor who preached from a pulpit and disappeared after service, not to resurface again until the next Sunday. He was a pastor who would shoot hoops with you in the gym—and if you were bold to challenge him to a game of "H.O.R.S.E.", you were definitely going to lose! No doubt about it. (He was a former all-American basketball player in college, who was even scouted by some professional teams...so let's just say he could play a little!) He was a perfect fit for a town like Beggs, Oklahoma. His messages were relatable, his faith was contagious, and his vision was to pastor the whole town—not to hide away inside the four walls and keep "having church" until Jesus comes.

Charletta wasn't just the typical "pastor's wife" who played the piano, led the women's ministry, and baked a mean corn casserole for the monthly church potluck. Rather, she was fun, relatable, always down to earth. Some of my fondest memories of those years were the times when I was invited to hang out with her and the kids, Amy and Andrew. Often on Sunday mornings and Wednesday nights, I would even swing by their house early before church started (which was easy because they lived in the parsonage next door), just so I could curl Amy's hair or help her get dressed. They let me be part of the family, and I loved it. I *longed* for it.

GOD CALLS REAL PEOPLE

It was under their leadership that one year at summer camp, at the age of 14, I heard God call me into ministry for the first time. And I believed it. Not because I felt worthy—but because they showed me that being real was enough.

Not long after, our youth pastor left the church for another opportunity, and Charletta was called upon to fill in during the interim. (*Regardless of the "interim" label, she was a natural at connecting with teenagers in a way that made them feel needed and known—and I was one of those teenagers.*) I couldn't believe what I was seeing: she was a woman doing ministry. Boldly. Authentically. She didn't pretend. She preached the gospel like she lived it—relatable, joyful, full

GROWING UP IN CHURCH, IF I'M HONEST, A LOT OF THE PASTORS I SAW DIDN'T SEEM REAL.

of Jesus. That was a revelation for me. Up until then, the only women I'd seen in ministry roles seemed untouchable, overly composed, or impossibly perfect. Charletta was none of those things. She was herself. And that gave me permission to believe I could be myself, too.

That's when I realized something I've never forgotten: **Authenticity is not a weakness—it's a witness.** It invites others to discover who they were made to be. It calls them out and calls them up. This is a guiding principle I have tried to live by, not only in my role as pastor, but as a wife, mother, and friend. When you think about it, this really shouldn't be that hard. Why should we invest all that energy trying to manage our reputation in this life…when all of this is not about us anyway? May the cry of my heart always be: **More of Him. Less of me.**

WORDS HAVE POWER

Here's what I know: your words carry weight. They have gravity. Substance. **Power**.

According to Proverbs 18:21, *"The tongue has the power of life and death."*

Just think about that for a moment. Every time you open your mouth—*every single time*—you're either speaking life or speaking death. Every word you speak has the ability to build someone up or tear them down. To heal or hurt. To inspire confidence or cut it off at the knees. Words can fuel the fire of someone's passion or put it out altogether. Whether through malice or carelessness—the intent doesn't nullify the impact—every word finds its way into the heart and accomplishes its work. There is no neutral ground. Every word has power.

I'm passionate about calling people into their God-given identity and helping them realize that their voice, their presence, their authenticity—it matters. You were never meant to shrink back. You were meant to shine! So show up as *you*, and speak like it counts—because it does.

Growing up in a house with six brothers as the only girl, life was… intense. Loud. Competitive. My brothers were all about sports—and so was I. My mom tried to balance the chaos by making me her little princess. She put me in dance classes early on, and I loved it—for five years. But as soon as I was old enough to pick up a basketball, I swapped the leotard for sneakers, and I never looked back.

THE STORY OF TWO COACHES

Basketball became my world. My coach, Coach Schachle, who also happened to be my actual uncle, was tough on me—harder than on anyone else, besides his daughter. I know now it was because he cared and wanted to see me excel, but he didn't speak life into me. On the contrary, more often than not, his words cut like a knife. His approach was to push through criticism, not encouragement. To be fair, that coaching method wasn't uncommon in those days, so I should probably cut him a little slack. After all, if he was trying to make me tougher, it worked. But that doesn't mean his words didn't hurt. Every one of them hit their mark.

In middle school, I was always stuck playing defense in Oklahoma's six-on-six system. Now if you've never heard of this style of basketball, a quick Google search might be helpful. But for the sake of context, let me explain the basic idea. Just imagine two separate three-on-three basketball games being played on opposite ends of the same court, at the same time. Crazy right? But here's the twist: there's only one ball. So, the ball passed back and forth across the halfcourt line—but none of the players ever did. (Confused yet?) Defensive players were exclusively on defense. They never had the opportunity to score...because they never crossed half court.

So, why is any of this important? Coach Schachle told me I couldn't shoot. I would never be a shooter. I just wasn't good enough to play offense. End of story.

But I was determined to prove him wrong. I started going to the gym before school. After school. At every summer camp I could find. Quietly grinding, working on my game, pushing myself to get better—because I *could* shoot. Even when my uncle kept me stuck on defense, I kept showing up. I didn't argue. I didn't boast. I just practiced.

And then came my freshman year. A new coach—Coach Alexander, (whom we called "Coach A")—stepped in, and everything changed. He *saw* me. Not just what I had been doing, but what I *could* do. He believed in me and gave me a shot at offense. I averaged 15 points a game that year— not because something magical happened, but because **everything I had been doing in secret was now coming to light.**

All those unseen hours? They mattered. They didn't stay hidden. My preparation met opportunity. My private persistence produced public fruit. And here's what I've learned—**that's not just basketball. That's life. That's Kingdom.**

The Bible puts it like this:

> *"For there is nothing hidden that will not be disclosed, and nothing concealed that will not be brought out into the open."*
> *— Luke 8:17 (NIV)*

That truth cuts both ways. The good stuff and the messy stuff—eventually, it all comes out. God is faithful to bring into the light what's been growing in the dark. Whether it's sin that needs healing, or obedience that's about to be rewarded, **what's done in the secret places shapes what gets revealed in public spaces.**

So keep showing up. Keep doing the work. Be real. Be faithful. Because sooner or later, what's been growing behind the scenes will step into the spotlight. And when it does, may it reveal the person God always knew you were becoming.

From that day forward, I played offense and loved every second. As it turned out, I guess I had the potential to be a pretty good shooter after all. *(Not to brag—well, maybe a little—but David wanted me to be sure and include the fact that I would eventually lead the state of Oklahoma in 3-pointers during my junior year. He was a ball player, too, so I guess he can appreciate all those hours in the gym.)*

FIVE MINUTES IN A FURNITURE STORE

In the process of writing this book, one particular experience came back to my mind which illustrates the power of words. On the surface, it was a seemingly insignificant interaction, but it made a profound impact upon me.

During my middle school years, not only did I play basketball, but I ran track as well. As a member of the team, I was expected to help raise funds for the summer track program, so I went around to local businesses in Okmulgee asking for support. One business owner, Bill Nigh—(*no, not the science guy*)—owned Jones Furniture Store. I was only 13 years old when I walked into his store, boldly asking him to write a big check to sponsor the track program. Bill listened to my passionate sales pitch, and then he told me something I'll never forget. He said, "*You are a leader. Anything you put your heart and mind into, you can do. Leadership is inside you.*"

Did I walk out of that store with a donation that day? You bet I did! Bill supported the team, but not because he cared about track. It was because he believed in *me*. He saw greatness in me—and he challenged me to walk in it. From Bill's perspective, this really wasn't about a donation—it was about destiny.

Words have power. They shape identity. They open doors. They water the seeds God has planted in people. Bill Nigh wasn't a teacher, coach, or family member. He was just someone paying attention. But he called out something in me that aligned with how God made me. I think about that a lot. How many people around us are waiting to hear words that call them forward? How many are unsure of their gifts because no one's ever affirmed them?

That day marked me. Isn't it CRAZY how one five-minute conversation in a furniture store has stayed with me for almost forty years?   Hard to believe…but **God is in the crazy.**

DECLARATION OF A SPIRITUAL LEADER: I LEAD FROM WHO I AM

We encourage you to speak this over yourself today. Then again tomorrow. And every day.

These words carry weight, because they're rooted in truth.

Say it boldly. Let it sink in. Believe it.

I am not called to impress—I am called to be authentic.

I am not performing for people—I am walking in purpose.

God anointed me—flawed, growing,
and filled with His Spirit.

I will not compare my voice, my journey,
or my calling to anyone else.

I lead best when I lead from who I truly am in Christ.

I declare that my authenticity is my superpower.

I do not hide my humanity—I let it testify of His grace.

I speak life over myself and over those I'm called to lead.

I reject perfectionism and embrace Spirit-led progress.

Even when I stumble, I fall forward—
because grace carries me.

My words are not empty—they are full of authority.

When I speak, heaven listens.

When I declare truth, darkness trembles.

When I lead authentically, people are set free.

I am a Kingdom leader.

I am real. I am called. In Christ, I am more than enough.

SPIRIT-EMPOWERED AUTHENTICITY

(DAVID:)

Not long ago, I heard a statement that caught my attention: *"Authenticity is the superpower of our day."*

On the surface, this appears to be a refreshing reminder to simply *Be yourself.* In other words, don't be like everyone else—just be yourself. You be you. Sounds harmless enough, but something about the idea kept bothering me. I couldn't shake the thought that these days it has become completely acceptable (and profitable) to *say* anything, *do* anything, and *be* anything in pursuit of popularity. And once you get the attention, now you have to keep it...at all costs. Gotta get clicks. Gotta get likes. Gotta give the people what they want.

Build your platform. Grow your following. Protect your image. Manage your brand. Call it whatever you want—but at the end of the day, it's all an act. A performance.

Unfortunately, sometimes this can even be true of those of us serving in ministry. If church leaders aren't mindful, we may find ourselves spending more time "posting" than praying. More concerned with image than integrity. After all, none of us are above to the gravitational pull of public adoration. In our flesh, we want it. Maybe *need* it. But may I remind you **we can't reach this world if we need this world.**

Here is the obvious problem with seeking the praise of men more than the praise that comes from God: **Jesus didn't live that way.** He lived surrendered. Submitted. Dependent on the voice of the Father to show him the next move. Everything he did was led by the Spirit. No hidden agendas. No perks along with his popularity. He chose to deflect praise, rather than bask in it. He humbled himself. He made himself nothing.

Do you see it? Jesus never drew attention away from the Father's redemptive plan. So, we're going to have to do things His way—not ours. Our calling has to be about making Him famous—not ourselves.

MORE THAN WORDS

Here's the challenge: it's not enough for Christians to talk about God, preach sermons, or communicate rules, guidelines, and lessons. All of that has a place—but the gospel was never meant to be communicated through words alone. It's meant to be embodied. Fleshed out. Personal. Real. There must be life on life. There must be relationship. That's the only way we can fully demonstrate the love and nature of God to a watching world.

2 Corinthians 5 says that God has given us the ministry of reconciliation—that He is actively reconciling the world to Himself through Christ. And now, we are His *ambassadors*. He is making His appeal through us. Think about that. God has chosen to use our lives as the canvas upon which He paints His love. We aren't just messengers—we're embodiments of the message.

The gospel cannot be shared by words alone. The message of hope must take on flesh—just like Jesus did. John 1 tells us, *"The Word became flesh and made His dwelling among us."* Jesus didn't just come to teach us things about God. He came to show us what God is like. To be God-with-us. Incarnational. That will require us, then, to live *incarnationally* too.

And so, if we are to be faithful in this calling—this ministry of reconciliation—we must follow His example. We must live differently than the world around us. We must be humble in a world driven by pride. Loving in a world bent on hate. Real in a world addicted to image.

But hear this: our lives cannot simply be good moral examples. We are not lifestyle influencers. We are *ambassadors*. Our lives must point to Jesus. He is the Word that became flesh. And now, our calling is to dwell among people in such a way that they see Him through us.

LIVING PROOF OF A LOVING GOD

Authenticity. Proximity. Presence. That's what reveals Christ. The world doesn't need more polished sermons—it needs people who carry the presence of Jesus into living rooms, classrooms, workplaces, and neighborhoods. People who show up, not just speak up. People who know what it means to be **Living proof of a loving God to a watching world.**

If we're going to truly carry out this ministry of reconciliation—authenticity alone won't be enough. It's not sufficient to simply "be present" in the lives of those who are hurting, confused, or far from God. We need something more—**Spirit-empowered authenticity**. The kind that brings both compassion and conviction, that moves beyond connection into transformation, where the presence of the Holy Spirit enables us to speak hope, live truth, and see lives set free.

1. Spirit-Empowered Authenticity Opens Doors for Real Conversations

You don't need to sound like someone else to carry power— you just need to sound like you. God anointed you, not a version of you trying to mimic someone else's highlight reel. In a world of performance, your authenticity is your secret weapon—it cuts through noise, inspires trust, and releases permission for others to be real too.

Spirit-empowered leaders declare who God says they are before it looks like it.

People aren't looking for perfect leaders—they're looking for real ones. They're not drawn to the ones who pretend to have it all together, but to the ones who stumbled, fell forward, and are honest about it. Authenticity doesn't make you weak—it makes you trustworthy. It shows people that the same God who's working in you can work in them too.

Words have power—especially when they come from a life surrendered to Christ. When you speak from your authentic self, aligned with the Spirit, your voice carries heaven's weight.

2. Spirit-Empowered Authenticity Carries Spiritual Authority

You don't just speak sermons—you speak into spiritual atmospheres. When your life is aligned with the Spirit, your words don't just inspire; *they shift things.* As a leader, your declarations have weight. Don't shrink back from speaking boldly what God has said because heaven moves on faith-filled words.

Words have power—not just emotionally, but spiritually. When you speak with kingdom authority, you're not just motivating people—you're breaking yokes, restoring hope, and activating purpose.

Your words are not just expressions; they are divine instruments.

3. Spirit-Empowered Authenticity Gives You Voice

When you model authenticity, you give others permission to drop the act and pick up their calling. You don't set people free by being untouchable—you set them free by being real, Spirit-filled, and full of grace. Authentic leaders speak to the potential, not just the present condition, in others.

You lead best not when you impress, but when you impart. Speak life over yourself first—and then over the generations watching you. Because words have power—and yours carry legacy.

Don't miss this.

Spirit-empowered authenticity is not just a cute idea. It's a powerful reality. When God's people "just show up"—letting our words be demonstrated through tangible acts of kindness—it's CRAZY what He will do through us.

Simply put: words are great—but action is better.

Never was this clearer to us than in the summer of 2022, when our church had an opportunity to host a camp for teenage foster kids. We had one idea in mind, but God had another.

What happened next was CRAZY...

ONE CRAZY CAMP STORY

Before we ever stepped foot on a campground in August 2022 to host a life-changing week with foster teens, the heart for this kind of ministry was already beating strong in our church.

Several years earlier, we'd launched Bridge Church Foster & Adoption Care Ministry—a vision we had been praying into and building toward for quite some time. With the help of our partners at Backyard Orphans, who trained and equipped us, we were beginning to gain some real traction. From hosting Parents Night Out events to give foster families a well-deserved break, to assembling specialized support teams—handymen, meal providers, prayer partners—we created a structure to surround those walking through the journey of fostering and adoption. As part of this ministry, we also looked for ways to serve and encourage CPS workers, recognizing their often unseen and thankless work. We hosted appreciation breakfasts, offered gift cards, and simply let them know they were seen and valued.

CRAZY QUESTION

It was in one of those early calls to the state—just wanting to honor a few caseworkers—that everything changed. After discussing a few of the proposals we had in mind, our contact person from the State office shifted the conversation. "Can we talk to you about something else?" That unexpected question opened the door to what would become one of the most powerful ministry moments I've ever experienced.

> *"Would you be interested in hosting a camp event for foster kids from across Texas?"*

And just like that, we were off and running. As the conversation continued, here's what we learned. Each year, the State of Texas designates part of their annual budget specifically for high-school age foster kids to be able to attend camps in the summer. However, due to the COVID-19 pandemic, all camps had been discontinued since 2020. This was now 2 years later, apparently if the designated camp funds were not spent by the end of 2022...they would be lost altogether. So, the State was asking us to spend their money. *(Yes, you read that correctly.)*

CRAZY BUDGET

Our next question (of course!) was, "So exactly how much money are we talking here?" The answer knocked us back in our seats: "Oh, about two million dollars."

Wow! With that much money available, the sky was the limit! *(Michele and I started dreaming BIG – how about flying all these kids to Cancun for a beach trip, or maybe a quick cruise to the Mediterranean, or even a ski trip to Aspen over Christmas break...if the funds were still available, of course! Obviously, none of those options would've ever gotten off the drawing board...but hey, a guy can dream, can't he?)*

Seriously though, our contact person told us that we should "shoot for the moon" with our budget. He said that whatever amount we could reasonably spend they would more than likely approve. The biggest challenge we were facing was time—we only had about 8 weeks to pull this thing together—so our team went to work.

It probably shouldn't have surprised me how quickly the details started falling into place—after all, our God specializes in the impossible—but sometimes I can be a slow learner, so I watched in amazement as He did what He always does.

Our first call was to Lakeview Camp, where all our church camp activities are held each year. They were, of course, thrilled to work with us. We knew they were going to do most of the heavy lifting—providing lodging, handling all the meals, coordinating team-building activities, setting up meeting rooms, and more—but in return, they would be generously compensated. In fact, we told them *not* to give us a discounted rate; since the state was footing the bill, we encouraged them to charge full price!

OUR GOD SPECIALIZES IN THE IMPOSSIBLE

Once the location was secured, things started moving even faster. T-shirts, backpacks and monogrammed journals were all designed and ordered. Inflatables and food trucks were reserved. Guest speakers were lined up. Bridge Church volunteers were recruited and trained. The logistics were massive—but our team hustled, made a plan, and executed it quickly.

But behind the scenes, one question was on everyone's minds: "How can we make a life-changing impact when we can't even speak the name of Jesus?"

CRAZY CAMP GUIDELINES

You see, although the state had been incredibly generous with allocating resources, their only stipulation was that this was *not* to be a faith-based camp in any way. We weren't allowed to preach, pray publicly, or have worship experiences. All of this felt very much outside our comfort zone—but this was nonnegotiable, so we pivoted. Instead of sermons, we gave motivational talks. Instead of praise, we played games. Instead of altar calls, we invited them to recite the following affirmations. It went something like this:

Hey everybody, repeat after me: "I rock! I'm awesome! I was made for more!" (they would speak over themselves)

OK, now turn to the person sitting next to you, and speak this over them:

"You rock! You're awesome! You were made for more!" (and they did)

Now, let's all say this together:
"We rock. We're awesome. We were made for more."

The entire atmosphere was one of authenticity. What made it real? We simply showed up. We were present. We were Jesus with skin on. Like St. Francis of Assisi said, "Preach the gospel at all times. If necessary, use words."

This camp reflected the very DNA of our church—to be *living proof of a loving God to a watching world*. It's the reason we named our church **The Bridge**. Based on Matthew 5:16, our mission is to let our light shine before others so they may see our good works and glorify God. When we serve authentically—when we smile, listen, give, and love—it creates a holy wonder. People don't glorify us. They glorify God. That's the point. That's the bridge.

The camp theme was **"Words Have Power."** And they did. In just 2.5 days, hearts opened. Girls poured out their stories to Michele during short rides on the golf cart—from tales of absent or incarcerated fathers, to stories of abuse and pain. They felt safe. They felt seen. One case worker after another told us the same thing: "*We've never seen these kids open up like this! Whatever you guys are doing…it's working. Thank you for making a difference.*"

CRAZY TEACHING MOMENT

And then there was the **milk crate story**.

In the outdoor tabernacle, a boy named Angel attempted the challenge of climbing a tall, unstable tower of milk crates—stacked two by two—each crate added as he climbed. The goal was to reach the top without the tower collapsing. He was harnessed in for safety, but it didn't lessen the drama. The higher he got, the more the crowd grew. Even though there was a lot going on at camp, people paused to watch him. The crates wobbled. People gasped, held their breath, and quietly cheered with each step higher. He didn't quite make it all the way to the top, but he climbed higher than anyone else. And when he finally fell, the crowd didn't make fun of him—they cheered!

Later that night, during the closing session, we gave the students space to share what they'd learned or what had impacted them. The responses were raw and powerful:

> *"No matter what my parents told me, I know I am not an accident."*
> *"I learned that I am beautiful, inside and out."*
> *"I know I'm worth it."*
> *"I rock. I'm awesome. I was made for more."*

As I was just about to wrap up the sharing time and bring the night to a conclusion, from the corner of my eye I saw a young man stand to his feet in the back of the room. It was Angel. All he said was, *"One day, I'm gonna make it out of the hood"* – and he sat back down. Several of his friends chuckled – and to be honest, it was hard to tell whether Angel was being serious or just entertaining his buddies. Judging by the reaction of the room—since they knew him better than we did—I assumed it was the latter. Either way, something about that moment suddenly felt different. In that moment, the Holy Spirit prompted me to have him stand again. A quiet hush fell over the room as everyone was curious to see what would happen next.

I reminded him (and the rest of the room) that he was the one who had climbed the crates. I said, *"You think you failed because you didn't reach the top. But you went higher than anyone else. We were watching. We were with you. And we cheered...even when you fell."*

I asked him to think back over what had happened earlier. I wanted him to do his best to remember that feeling of people cheering for him, urging him on. I wanted there to be no mistake there were people who believed in him. Then, I felt the Spirit nudge me to go one step further...

From across the room, I locked eyes with him and said, *"Angel, I want you to know something...you WILL get out of the hood one day. There is no doubt in my mind—it's going to happen! Not because I said so, but because YOU did... and I believe your words have power."*

My voice broke as I felt the gravity of the moment. Even though I wasn't permitted to mention the name Jesus, there was no doubt He was the One speaking directly to Angel's heart. I could see tears welling up in the young man's eyes as he listened intently.

"And you know what's even more awesome? Because of the words you've spoken here today—not only will your life be different, but the lives of your children, too. And yes,

even your grandchildren will have a different future because of this very moment. Never forget that your words have power. THIS. CHANGES. EVERYTHING."

That was the moment everyone on our team carried home. We couldn't believe how impactful it was just to show up. God provided the funding. He paved the way. He was in every detail—because He values authenticity and presence. The kids were blessed. The caseworkers were blessed. Even the campground staff were blessed. All because we chose to be real. To show up. To be the living proof of a loving God to a watching world.

And when you do that, God shows up in ways you can't predict.

Because **God is always in the crazy.**

(By the way, for those who might be wondering, "So…how close did you guys get to spending the whole two million?" Well, as it turns out, it's harder than you think to spend un-limited cash in 8 weeks, but we did the best we could. The grand total for Bridge Summer Camp was $137,000—not too shabby for two-and-a-half days, huh? Of course, the best part is…we didn't pay a dime! We just sat back and watched in amazement as our GOD took care of it all—it just so happens he used the State of Texas to write the check.

THE WORLD IS WATCHING

So here's where it all comes together: **Be real. Be authentic. Speak life.** Not just because it's trendy, but because it's *transformational.* God doesn't move through who we pretend to be—He moves through who we truly are. Your behind-the-scenes obedience, your quiet consistency, your whispered prayers—they all matter. They're building something real. And one day, what's been cultivated in secret will rise to the surface and speak for itself. Let your life tell the truth. Let your words carry heaven's authority. Let your leadership come not from perfection, but from presence.

This world doesn't need more polished performances—it needs Spirit-filled people who dare to lead with authenticity and speak with holy fire. So keep showing up, keep sowing in the dark, and keep being you. Because in Christ, the *real you* is more than enough. And when you lead from that place? Lives are changed. Legacy is formed. Kingdom comes.

Be real—and watch what God will do.

PRACTICAL TAKEAWAYS

» **Practice Integrity in the Secret Place**

What you do when no one is watching prepares you for when everyone is. Whether it's discipline, prayer, or character—hidden faithfulness leads to public fruit.

» **Speak Life Like It Matters—Because It Does**

Your words can break someone or build them. Don't underestimate the impact of one moment of encouragement. Say what calls people higher.

» **Be Authentically You**

You were never called to be a copy. Stop comparing. Your authentic self is the most powerful tool in God's hands. When you're real, others find the courage to be real too.

» **Recognize Your Hidden Season Is Sacred**

Just because it's unseen doesn't mean it's unimportant. God does some of His best work in the unseen places. Don't despise the waiting room—He's preparing you for the platform.

REFLECTION QUESTIONS

Use these for personal reflection, couple conversations, or your leadership circle.

1.   Who are you when no one's watching?
What habits, words, or thoughts dominate your private world? Are they preparing you for the future God has for you?

2.   Do your words reflect heaven's values?
Are you speaking life into your children, spouse, friends, coworkers—or are your words pulling them down?

3.   In what areas have you been tempted to perform or pretend?
What would it look like to show up more authentically in those spaces?

4.   Who spoke life into you when you needed it most?
How did their words impact you—and how can you now be that voice for someone else?

5.   Is there anything you need to bring into the light?
Whether it's hidden sin or a hidden strength, what needs to be exposed so that growth can happen?

BETTER TOGETHER

IF YOU WANT TO GO FAST,
GO ALONE. IF YOU WANT TO
GO FAR, GO TOGETHER.
(AFRICAN PROVERB)

"THE CHURCH IS NOT A
COLLECTION OF LOOSE
INDIVIDUALS;
IT'S A NEW HUMANITY,
A FAMILY, A BODY.
WE'RE MADE FOR ONE ANOTHER."

(TIM KELLER)

CHAPTER 5:
MICHELE:

Ministry is a marathon—not a sprint.

Back in 2012, David had decided to run a marathon. If you've ever trained for one, you know the number one rule of marathon running is: **Finish!** No matter what happens, no matter what setbacks you face, no matter how slow you go—you just keep moving forward. Period. Quitting is not an option. You have to settle that in your heart *before* you ever step up to the starting line. I *will* finish.

He had trained diligently over nearly four months, so he felt ready for race day. His running partner that day was our friend, Todd Davis. He was only planning to run the half-marathon (13.1 miles), but David wanted to complete the full 26.2-mile race. He started off strong. Thanks to the electronic chip attached to his shoe, I could keep track of his progress throughout the entire race.   Around mile 13 or 14, David started cramping—first his legs, then his arms. It was bad. He would later tell me it felt like his whole body was shutting down. At mile marker 15, where I was supposed to meet him, he didn't show. By that point in the race, he was already over an hour behind pace, so I knew something was wrong. That's when I decided to go back to the car, drive to a different checkpoint, and see if I could locate him.

When I finally spotted him, it was obvious he was really struggling. He wasn't running. He wasn't jogging. He was barely walking—more of a limp than anything else. (It was pretty pitiful, to be honest.) In spite of his training, it didn't look like he would be able to continue.

So I did something crazy – I decided to join him. (He was already so far back from the pack, that the roads were pretty wide open anyway. I just stepped out into the street and started walking with him. After a few minutes, I said, "Hey, let's try to jog to that stop sign. You ready?" He did it, then we walked a while. A little later, "Now let's jog to the next light pole." You get the idea. And that's how we kept going—one stop sign, one light pole, one mile at a time.

What was supposed to be just a couple of miles turned into the final stretch of the race. From mile 16 to mile 26, it wasn't about how fast we were going. It was about not quitting. And that's how David finished the race. That's how **we** finished the race.

We crossed the finish line...*together*.

Not because the pain went away. Not because the path got easier. But because he knew the #1 rule of marathons. Finish! Quitting is not an option. And when his strength was gone, his companion wasn't. He needed me that day—just like I've needed him, countless times before and after that day.

This race of life—this race of ministry—is a marathon.

It's not glamorous. It's stop signs and light poles. It's obedience in inches. It's grace for today, strength for the next step. And it's that kind of faithfulness that God honors and multiplies.

It's **little by little...until.**

And I'm grateful David and I get to run together. It's better that way.

In this chapter, we want to share some of the ways we have lived out this "Better Together" principle. Our hope is that as you read, you will discover the value of doing life together:

1.   MARRIAGE AND CO-PASTORING

First, a disclaimer: We understand that not all couples in ministry are called to serve as *co-pastors*. This is not for everybody. In fact, earlier in our marriage, this probably wouldn't have been advisable for us either. In that season, we were still learning about our own leadership styles, our giftings, and how to work best together. Plus, with four daughters running around the house, there didn't seem to be a lot of "extra" time to explore new out-of-the-box church leadership models. So, we just did what we knew.

Not to mention that back in those days, healthy models for this type of collaborative ministry were not common, if there were any at all, within our ministry context. To be clear, this is referring to husband and wife teams who were co-leading their local church. If they were out there, we certainly didn't know where to find them! However, in God's timing we came to believe that this was how He wanted us to lead our church.

That shift did not happen overnight. There were some bumps in the road along the way. Even as we share some of our experiences in this chapter, you will see there was an adjustment period in the early days of our co-pastoring journey. Thankfully, we kept learning, kept growing, and eventually began to find our stride.

To be clear, we have always done ministry together. God called **both** of us—long before we even knew each other—to devote our lives to sharing the Gospel and serving the Church. We **both** responded to that call, individually, in our own ways. We **both** attended Bible college to prepare ourselves for whatever God had in store. Michele's degree was in elementary education, David's was in church leadership. Presently we are **both** credentialed ministers with the Assemblies of God, although that was not always the case. David became an ordained minister in 1998. Michele didn't feel a need to pursue her credentials until a few years ago—but she was *always* called. As a school teacher, then stay-at-home mom, then business owner, she wore lots of other hats. Adding "licensed minister" to her resume didn't feel very necessary—after all, she was already doing it, with or without the word "Reverend" on a plastic card in her wallet. Eventually, the Holy Spirit nudged her to complete the process, so that's what she did. The certificate on the wall was a nice addition, but her obedience to the call began when she said "YES" at a summer camp over thirty years ago.

We have **both** developed our own spiritual disciplines in the areas of prayer, Bible study, journaling, worship, fasting, spiritual community and serving in the church.

(By the way, this is really important. It's hard to be effective as co-pastors if only one of you is fully committed to the task of hearing from God and doing what He says. There will undoubtedly be times when you will need to lean into one another's discernment, because the Lord may be speaking to him/her, not you. In those moments, you'll be thankful for a spouse who not only prays and reads the Bible, but who also helps carry the prophetic leadership mantle upon both of you.)

In other words, we are **both** bought in. For the first twenty-four years of marriage, we both knew we were in this together. All in. Even though neither of us were raised in pastor's homes, we had been around the church world long enough to learn a few things about the stress of ministry. It can be a grind. Marriage can be challenging enough—but when you add the burden and responsibility of leading a church, it brings a whole different kind of tension into the relationship.

Then in 2018, we entered into a new season as co-pastors. This was not an easy transition for us, but it has been worth it. In this section, we thought it would be helpful (or at the very least, entertaining) to "pull back the curtain" and share more details about how this transition came about— the good, the bad, and the ugly. We will each share our separate versions of the story, and then you can decide which one of us to believe. *(We're totally kidding...or are we?)*

In all seriousness, if you're a couple considering whether co-pastoring is for you, our hope is that by sharing both of our perspectives, you'll find clarity, encouragement, and maybe even the courage to step into the water and see what God will do.

THE STORY BEHIND THE STORY

(MICHELE:)

My journey to co-pastoring alongside David didn't begin with a microphone or a platform—it began with grief, mentorship, business, obedience, and the kind of yes that requires everything. Through it all, God was writing a bigger story. One rooted in the truth that we really are... better together.

2017 was marked by deep loss. People who had spoken into our lives—mentors, friends, spiritual parents—passed away. It was a year of mourning. But also a year of divine whispers. God was asking me for more than the usual yes. He was calling me to a committed yes—a "yes, no matter what it costs." Yes **period**.

Looking back, I realize He had been preparing me all along. For 13 years, I had led in business. I discipled women in boardrooms and living rooms. What looked like entrepreneurship was actually equipping. God had used those years to build leadership in me—firm, Spirit-filled, faith-forward leadership.

So when David and I started seriously talking about co-pastoring in early 2018, it wasn't a brand-new idea. We had been ministering together for years—I just operated behind the scenes. Kids ministry. Organization. Strategy. Silent strength. But God began speaking: **This season will look different**. And that meant stepping forward—not just supporting, but co-leading. God didn't need my understanding. He needed my obedience. So I kept on praying and waited to see when (or if) David would take the lead—but he never did.

One night as we were lying in bed, having yet another conversation about this same topic—but still with no action steps anywhere on the horizon—I was done waiting. I rolled over, look David in the eyes, and asked, "When are you going to talk to the board about this?"

David hesitated. In that moment, I had a sudden realization: it wasn't the board holding him back, it was fear. Insecurity. Control. The unknown of what it would look like to lead with someone like me. Bold, decisive, driven. I could see it in his eyes, and in that moment I said what was true but painful: *"You're the one* who's not ready for me to be co-pastor."

And I turned over with tears in my eyes.

When I'm processing pain, I go quiet—because I know words have weight, and I didn't want to speak from a place of hurt. But in the silence, God met me. He reminded me: This calling isn't conditional on anyone else's approval. Say yes to Me, and I'll take care of the rest.

So I told David, *"I know God's calling me to something new. I thought it would be alongside you. But if not, I'll still say yes."*

That moment shifted something.

I wasn't trying to hurt him, but I couldn't be quiet anymore. The next words out of my mouth hit him hard—and in that moment, I *meant* them.

I spoke very calmly, but my tone let him know how serious I was.

I told him, "Well at least now I know why this has been such a struggle. It's *you*. You're the one who doesn't want this. So here's what's going to happen: I'm stepping back. I know God is wanting to do something new in my life—and I wanted it to be here in the church, serving with you—but I guess God has a different plan for me. That makes me sad. Don't worry, I'll still attend church on Sundays, and I will support you…but I need to step back for a while, so I can figure out what all of this means."

David tried to apologize, of course, but in that moment, I really didn't want to hear anything he had to say. His actions had already spoken. Now he was just trying to make things better, but the damage had been done. I meant what I said. I needed time to process.

The next day, David made a phone call to Pastor Jim Hennesy, a mentor in our life who had modeled co-leadership with his wife, Becky. They talked about what it meant to lead together without fear, without comparison, and without competition. I'll let David share the rest of that conversation, because that's really his story, not mine.

Here's what I know: When David came back, he was vulnerable and real. He sincerely apologized for letting his insecurity get in the way. Naturally, I forgave him (*although I didn't want to let him off the hook too easily*). From that day forward, we truly began leading in a new way—each with our distinct strengths, but with one heart and one mission.

(DAVID:)

I remember that night like it was yesterday! It was awful. (..and so were the next few days, as we sorted out the emotions, assessed the damage, and got to work on repairing the trust I had broken.) This wasn't just a fight; it was a defining moment. I didn't just make Michele mad—I wounded her spirit. This was a big deal, and I knew it.

So the next day, I reached out to a mentor of mine, Jim Hennesy. He and his wife, Becky, are pastors of Trinity Church, where they have served together for many years. Thankfully, he had a few minutes to talk, so I just jumped right into the deep end! When I had finished explaining the situation—(otherwise known as "dumping" on him)—he shared some practical wisdom from their years of marriage and ministry.

Here's what he told me:

1. **First, you need to apologize (again).** I had already done that, of course, but he told me to get a little more specific! Take full ownership. No excuses. Admit your insecurity, or selfishness, or whatever else is going on in your heart.

2. **Whatever Becky touches, she makes better.** The anointing that is upon her life blesses every area of our church. So why would I try to limit that, or contain her influence?

He said this in response to the battery of questions I had been asking him, most of which sound utterly ridiculous in hindsight:

Who should I have Michele report to?

Where will she fit on the organizational chart?

What should her specific "portfolio" include?

How should we explain to the staff they now have 2 bosses instead of 1? Should she have required office hours?

Does she need an office of her own? Or are we going to share one?

He challenged me not to get bogged down in details that don't matter. These are only distractions. Whatever area of the church Michele touches will be better because of her influence and anointing.

3.   Every family is healthiest when it has both a mom and a dad. So, why should a church family be different? Lots of churches value the role of the "spiritual father" for the house, but don't inherently see the same value in a spiritual **mother**. This needs to change—and since God is already preparing Michele's heart for this new season, it seems like a perfect opportunity to shift the culture. Your church family needs a mom!

Lastly, I told him I was basically feeling insecure and threatened by Michele's strong will, strong opinions, strong leadership style… (key word: *strong*). I told him that I knew it sounded crazy, but what if people in the church think she's a better leader than me? Or what if she doesn't like the way I'm leading, and tries to lead in her own way? (*Again, this sounds ridiculous, even as I type…because it's not like Michele was going to lead some kind of coups to overthrow me!*). She didn't want to takeover—she just wanted to make things better! She didn't want to get rid of me—she wanted to work alongside me.

YOUR CHURCH FAMILY NEEDS A MOM!

So, this was Pastor Jim's last word of wisdom—and it's so good:

4.   Your gifts are complementary, not contradictory. You are seeing only the differences between the two of you—not the unique strengths and giftings you both individually bring to the table. Imagine two different visuals: First, think of two closed fists hitting each other—this is **contradictory**. Next, picture two hands with interlocking fingers—this is **complementary**. The former is a problem; the latter is a perfect fit.

As I listened to those principles, the Holy Spirit settled my heart. Before we ended the call, Pastor Jim offered to pray over me and encouraged me to see God's hand in all of this. Then he said, "I'm excited to see what happens in this coming season. If you need me anytime, just call." He will never know how God used him that day.

BENEFITS OF CO-PASTORING

Ecclesiastes 4:9–12 paints a vivid picture of the strength found in partnership. It reminds us that two are better than one—not just for productivity, but for support, resilience, and shared strength in every season.

> *9 Two are better than one,*
> *because they have a good return for their labor:*
> *10 If either of them falls down,*
> *one can help the other up.*
> *But pity anyone who falls*
> *and has no one to help them up.*
> *11 Also, if two lie down together, they will keep warm.*
> *But how can one keep warm alone?*
> *12 Though one may be overpowered,*
> *two can defend themselves.*
> *A cord of three strands is not quickly broken.*

For us, it all comes down to one word: **SHARING**. In our roles as co-pastors, "better together" means sharing the work, sharing the weight, and sharing the wins. Let's briefly discuss each of them below:

SHARE THE <u>WORK</u>

(DAVID:)

> » **Time management –** Simply, because there are two of us, we can "divide and conquer!" This cuts down on duplication, because we don't have to be at all the same meetings and have all the same conversations. We can pick-and-choose the areas we are most passionate about, or best suited to handle. *(Now occasionally, we forget to tell each other all the decisions we made… so there are a few surprises along the way! I guess you could say that just keeps things exciting.)*

> » **Staff meetings –** We meet with our entire team every Tuesday morning. Typically, we are both there—and we both lead aspects of the meeting. However, if one of us is gone, the meeting can still happen. (Michele's meetings probably go faster than when I'm there…so the team never complains when I'm gone!)

> » **Sunday services –** Although I do most of the preaching, Michele still speaks multiple times during the year. If/when there is a conflict requiring one of us to be away, the other will hold down the fort.

SHARE THE <u>WEIGHT</u>

Ministry carries a weight that's hard to describe—one that's often only fully understood by those who've walked in it. There's a gravity that comes with pastoring—caring for people's souls, navigating leadership decisions, and carrying burdens that aren't always visible to others. That's why sharing the weight is so vital.

By the way, this isn't just a co-pastoring thing—it's true of marriage in general. In any healthy home, roles are shared. Someone handles the bills, someone mows the lawn, someone registers the kids for soccer or plans the family vacation. Every task may not be equally divided, but the load is shared with mutual respect and teamwork.

In ministry, that same principle applies. It's a gift to have someone walking beside you in the daily grind—someone who understands the demands and doesn't just support you, but shoulders it with you. When a late-night phone call comes in, you don't carry the emotional weight alone. When financial pressures arise or a hard leadership decision looms, you have a partner in the tension. And when your heart aches from betrayal, broken dreams, or tough conversations, it helps to know someone is right there, feeling it too.

Sharing the weight doesn't make the burden disappear—but it makes it bearable. And more than that, it reminds us we were never meant to carry it alone.

Share the WINS.

It's not just the weight that feels different when you're co-pastoring—it's the wins. There's something incredibly meaningful about getting to celebrate life change, growth, and breakthrough *together*. We get a front-row seat to see lives transformed, marriages restored, teams growing stronger, and people stepping into their calling. Our staff and leaders get the benefit of both spiritual parents—two pastors who love them, invest in them, and champion them every step of the way.

Another incredible win has been **watching women step into their God-given calling**. Michele's leadership has given them both *permission* and a *pathway*—not just to dream about ministry, but to walk confidently in it. They have a model to follow and a voice reminding them they are seen, valued, and called.

And then there's our greatest joy: **watching our own kids walk into their callings**. Our oldest daughter, **Madison**, serves as our youth pastor. **Macy**, our second daughter, leads worship and production. Both girls earned degrees in church ministry and leadership—and now they're leading with us, along with their husbands. **Mackenzie**, our third daughter, led the youth worship team, and she will begin Bible college to pursue her call. And **Madelyn**, our youngest, has a bold passion for sharing God's word. We're watching our kids grow up not just *around* ministry—but *in ministry*. This is what dreams are made of. Doing life and leadership with the people you love most—these are the wins we'll never take for granted.

5.   LEADERSHIP TEAM

(MICHELE:)

Ministry isn't just about sharing the gospel—it's about sharing our lives with the people God called us to serve. Notice how clearly the apostle Paul states this in his first letter to the Thessalonian believers:

> *"Because we loved you so much, we were delighted to share with you not only the gospel of God but our lives as well."* (1 Thessalonians 2:8)

How could it be any clearer than that? As church leaders, we aren't simply called to preach truth from the pulpit. Obviously that's important, but it doesn't stop there. We are also called to live among the people we lead. Share the gospel *and* your life. Not either/or. It's both/and.

Over the years, this simple biblical principle has shaped not only our church culture, as a whole, but the way we cultivate community within our leadership team. That's why we take our hiring process seriously. We don't rush. We're not just filling roles—we're creating family. But not just the kind of family who sits around the campfire singing kumbaya—we're the kind of family that wants to make a difference around the block and around the world. We want to get stuff done. We don't have time to waste. So we look for people who fit the culture we are building—those not afraid to work hard, but also ready to play hard.

One of David's mentors once challenged him: *"Don't ever hire someone on your team who you wouldn't want to hang out with after work."* At first that sounded strange, but over the years we came to understand. He was basically saying, don't hire them if you don't even like them! Not to make this weird, but is there chemistry? Do you feel a connection? If not, you should probably keep looking. *(Now, don't worry, this doesn't mean you'll have to go on all your vacations together, or take three-day road trips once a year just to have some good bonding time! But if you can't stand to see their face outside of office hours...there might be a problem.)*

We truly love our Bridge Church leadership team—and from time to time, we like to remind them: "You're here by *choice*, not by *chance*. Yes, God *called* you, but we *chose* you." And even though *words have power*, we look for tangible ways to show them as well. Here are a few of the fun things we've done to mix things up from time to time:

» **"Peace Shoes"** – For Pastor Appreciation Month (October) we like to take our team shopping for shoes. They get to pick out any pair they want (there's a price limit, of course, because we're not buying Air Jordans for everybody! Last I checked, Bridge Church is not being sponsored by any athletic apparel companies.) To keep things "spiritual," we refer back to the armor of God, and remind them, "everywhere you go, your feet are covered in the gospel of peace."

» **Easter Egg Hunt** – We've started a new tradition on Easter Sunday mornings, and I think it's here to stay: we host a staff-only egg hunt at 7:00am. (This is fun, of course, but it has the added benefit of making sure they arrive at church on-time!) The eggs they hunt for are filled with money, gift cards, dinner with the pastors, and everyone's favorite: coupons for a free day off.

» **7-Minute Challenge –** In keeping with the shopping vibe, we once took the team on a surprise trip to Target. When they arrived, we gave them 7 minutes to spend $70 on anything at all! There were only 3 rules: 1) You can't shop for anyone but yourself. For example, moms are not allowed to buy baby diapers. 2) No gift cards— you have to actually pick something out under pressure. That is part of the challenge. It's no fun if everyone just buys gift cards and shops on their own at a later time—we want to see the stress, the tears, and the epic meltdowns! 3) If you're even one second late, you get nothing. Then we synchronized our watches, and…GO! (Talk about CRAZY? That was a day we still laugh about.)

At the end of the day, all the surprises, celebrations, and spontaneous fun—those aren't just about money. They're about building a sense of closeness and shared purpose. We want our team to clearly understand that we're all in this together…and we wouldn't have it any other way! So don't get caught up in whether you can fund a big retreat or hand out expensive gifts. That's not the point. The point is to show value. To communicate love. To remind your team that they matter—that their presence, their calling, and their friendship are deeply appreciated. Ministry is better when it's not just work—it's family. And when your team knows they're loved, they'll give their best, not out of obligation, but out of joy. Because we really are better together.

6.   LIFE-GIVING FRIENDSHIPS

One of the deepest convictions we carry is this: You cannot lead in isolation. You must protect your circle. You must surround yourself with truth-tellers who know Scripture and walk in integrity. That's why we have told our kids for years: *"Show me your friends, and I'll show you your future."*   If this principle is good for teenagers, it's good for adults. Peer pressure doesn't stop when we graduate high school. It still matters who we spend time with.

In an effort to keep this super practical, let me take it one step further. Ask yourself this question: *"Who are your five closest friends?"* Go ahead, take a minute to create a list in your head. When you're ready, read this next statement... but brace yourself for some potentially hard truth. Whether you agree or disagree, at first, I hope you will reflect on the principle and think about your own life.

You are the average of the five people you spend the most time with.

Protect that circle. Make sure they speak God's Word— not just opinion. Make sure their private life is as solid as their public one. Do our closest friends have healthy marriages? Do they love Jesus? Do they attend church faithfully (assuming they're not pastors, in which case I would hope the answer is yes!) Do they manage their money well? Do they live with genuine humility?

The people closest to you are either sharpening you or wearing you down. There is no neutral. So chose your friends wisely. Surround yourself with those who challenge you to grow, live with integrity, and chase after the things of God, because over time, their influence will be seen in your life, one way or another.

Are your current friends raising your average...or bringing it down? That's for you to decide.

7.   LIKE-MINDED PASTORS & CHURCHES

(DAVID:)

Michele and I love spending time with other pastors. In fact, many of our longest lasting friendships are with people in ministry—not because we planned it that way, but because we just have a lot in common. We walk similar paths, face similar challenges, and celebrate similar wins. There's an unspoken understanding among pastors—the exhilaration of a Sunday that went well, and the discouragement of one that didn't. We've all been there, done that. There's a reason people say Monday morning is when most pastors feel like quitting. And yet, time and time again, I've been lifted by the encouragement of fellow pastors in my life. Sometimes we don't want to talk about church at all—we just grab coffee, play a round of golf, or share dad jokes.

When I first moved to Austin in 2003, I was invited to join something called a P.I.C. Group (it stands for *Pastors in Covenant*). All across the city, pastors met in groups of 4-7 to pray, laugh, and do life together. In my group, we were all from different denominations and varying levels of experience. Once a month, we gathered in someone's home, and it was life giving. We shared our highs and lows, prayed for each other's churches, and got to know one another's families. We quickly became brothers, and that group became a lifeline to me.

YOU ARE THE AVERAGE OF THE FIVE PEOPLE YOU SPEND THE MOST TIME WITH.

Later, when our church transitioned to Pflugerville, I connected with a new circle of pastors, this time meeting monthly for lunch and rotating between each other's churches. We laughed, we listened, we prayed. Once again, the connection was what I needed. Want to hear the coolest part of all? Any time Bridge Church broke ground on a building project—which has happened twice in the last ten years—these local pastors showed up to celebrate with us! They stood on stage to publicly support what God was doing. In a world that sometimes sees churches as competition, their presence sent a different message—one of unity, not rivalry. It was a powerful moment, not just for me, but for our church family.

When pastors come together—across denominations, backgrounds, and neighborhoods—something supernatural happens. We model the kingdom. We reflect Jesus. We are, truly, better together.

8.   COACHING

I first met Chris Sonksen in 2019 on a pastors' vision trip to El Salvador, where I'd been invited by my friend, Jason Dickenson. The purpose of the trip was to see the work being done through Convoy of Hope—things like their feeding programs and agricultural initiatives. But the unexpected blessing of that trip was meeting Chris. I still remember our first one-on-one conversation during dinner one night. From the start, he showed a genuine and sincere interest in our church. And every sentence he spoke seemed loaded with wisdom—as Michele likes to say, "Chris was dropping gold!" True to Chris Sonksen form, he was fast-talking and full of energy, but everything he shared was meaningful and packed with truth.

There was one statement in particular that stuck with me:

> **"Professionals get coaching. Amateurs learn by trial and error."**

It's a simple truth that shows up everywhere—from golf and baseball to music and film. The best in every field have coaches: swing coaches, pitching coaches, vocal coaches, acting coaches. Why? Because growth isn't automatic—it's intentional. And the same applies to pastors and church leaders. If we want to grow in our calling, we have to decide: do we want to be amateurs—learning by trial and error, taking the long way around—or professionals who are willing to invest in coaching? Choosing to grow means choosing to pay for growth. It's not just about investing in your church or your ministry; it's about investing in yourself.

And while there's nothing wrong with the amateur path, just know it's going to take longer. Coaching accelerates what God is already doing in you. It's putting your money where your mouth is—and saying, "I'm serious about the call of God on my life."

Toward the end of that meal, Chris leaned over and said, "Hey, if there's ever anything I can do to serve you or your church, it would be my honor." Looking back, I didn't even really know who he was—but I genuinely felt he meant it. There was no sales pitch, no pressure—just sincere generosity.

It took several months before we followed up, but eventually Michele and I set up a call to learn more about the coaching he offered. And in the years since, I can honestly say that everything I sensed in that first conversation was spot on. Chris truly loves the local church. He cares deeply about pastors and is passionate about helping them reach their God-given potential. He has poured his life into this calling, and we're living proof of the impact that calling can have.

As you may have guessed, we did move forward and hired him as our coach—and it's been one of the best investments we've ever made, both personally and for our church. His wisdom has sharpened our focus, expanded our vision, and helped us restructure our team and values. We're now aligned around becoming a multiplying, multi-site church. That's our vision—and Chris has been instrumental in helping us get there.

So why am I sharing about our personal coaching journey in a chapter called "Better Together"? Because the truth is, over the past few years, we've grown—not just through the wisdom we've received from our coach—but through the relationships and collaborations that have come from it. One of the things I appreciate most about Chris's approach is that he's not positioning himself as some kind of "ministry Yoda." He's a connector. His goal isn't just to coach pastors individually, but to build a network of like-minded leaders who can learn from one another and grow together.

Through his influence, we've participated in pastor summits and gatherings—places where real relationships are formed and where ministry leaders are encouraged, challenged, and equipped. These connections have sharpened our calling and clarified our mission. In fact, they've even led to the birth of a movement we're honored to be a part of: **Church Rescue Network**. This network is mobilizing pastors from across the country to invest their time, talent, and treasure into helping struggling churches. Our heart is simple—we want to rescue churches and coach pastors. That vision, and our role in it, came from a growing awareness: **we can't do ministry alone.**

Michele and I are fully committed to this. We want to grow. We want to link arms with others. And we want to be part of something bigger than ourselves. Because when pastors stand together, churches get stronger. And when churches get stronger, communities are transformed.

OUR VISION FOR MULTI-SITE MINISTRY

 US:

We've begun to see the fruit of this vision in real and tangible ways at Bridge Church. As we've embraced the coaching and training, our church has stepped more fully into our calling to be a multiplying, multi-site church. In 2022, we launched our first campus—**Bridge Bilingual**. This campus was born out of a desire to create a worship experience where both Spanish- and English-speaking families could attend church together in the same room, at the same time, sharing the same Spirit-filled atmosphere. It wasn't just a good idea; it was a vision birthed in the heart of our church and aligned with who we're called to be. That was the first campus we planted from within our church.

Then in 2024, God opened another door—this time to partner with a church in Austin. The pastors, whom we've known and loved for many years, reached out for help. Like many churches post-COVID, theirs had never fully recovered in terms of attendance or health, and they were facing real challenges. Initially, they simply asked if we could support them as a "missions project." Their building needed repairs, and they hoped we could send some people and resources to come alongside them for a short season. That's where it started.

But as the conversations deepened, something more began to take shape. After time, prayer, and honest dialogue, they expressed a desire to go beyond partnership—they wanted to become part of Bridge Church. Our plan was to "adopt" them—this would mean serving as their "parent church" and helping them find new strength and structure under the Bridge Church banner. So we entered a season of intentional meetings—with their leadership, with denominational leaders, and with our own team—and slowly but surely, God gave us favor to move forward. It was a year-long process, but finally at the start of 2025, it became official: they are now part of the Bridge Church family. We call them our **Bridge Church SOCO Campus** (which stands for South Congress, where the church is located)—and it has been such a joy to see that congregation come back to life! Plus, we get the privilege of walking out this journey hand-in-hand with our friends. It's just another example of how this "better together" mindset isn't just theory—it's becoming reality.

So what does it actually look like to move from a traditional church model to a multi-site vision? Well, that's the million-dollar question, isn't it? Plenty of books have been written on the topic, and there's far more we could say than fits in a single chapter. But here's what we've discovered— **it's a learning curve**. A big one. We've had to rethink nearly everything: service times, staffing structures, building logistics, coordination across campuses, and all the behind-the-scenes nuts and bolts. It's a lot of work—but we are better together.

We share resources. We share best practices. We even share things like theme decorations—Mother's Day, Father's Day, Easter, Christmas—it's one design, used across all campuses. We share sermon prep, leadership insights, and even the way we show honor. Our leaders and volunteers across all campuses come together three times each year for shared celebrations and moments of recognition.

(DAVID:)

Lastly, I want to highlight one specific benefit of our multi-site strategy —**the opportunity to develop people.** Michele always says it this way, "We're not trying to build a big church—we want to build big people." What's powerful is how this model creates space for the next generation of leaders. In today's world, many young, aspiring pastors feel called by God but are hesitant to go it alone. The idea of planting a church from scratch can feel overwhelming—but what we're able to give them is covering, coaching, and community. We give them a family to belong to, and a foundation to build on.

As we continue to pray into our next campus—and the one after that—we're learning, growing, and staying obedient to God's call. We truly believe the Church is still God's plan for reaching the world. And as long as there's ONE MORE person who needs to know Jesus, we'll keep showing up, keep building, and keep saying YES to what He's asking of us. Because we really are better together.

SOME CLOSING THOUGHTS...

MICHELE:

In 2018, when the Lord called us to begin leading *together* in a more intentional way, we had no way of knowing where it would lead. Co-pastoring was uncharted territory for us—new, different, and challenging—but we are grateful we said YES. Today, David and I still have so much to learn, but we thank God every day that we *get to do this…together.*

And to think… **it almost never happened.**

Why?

Because words have power.

Because people sometimes don't know what they're doing.

Because one unexpected conversation nearly destroyed this dream before we ever had a chance to chase after it.

In 2005, years before any of this "co-pastoring" stuff was even on our radar, David and I found ourselves sitting across the dinner table from a couple who had made the decision to leave our church. Since they had served in leadership roles, David requested a meeting to give them an opportunity to share their concerns. I think he hoped they would reconsider, but it became obvious pretty early in the evening that their mind was already made up. (In hindsight, the whole dinner was probably a bad idea, but we were young and naïve—and David just thought this was what pastors were "supposed" to do with disgruntled church members)

So there we sat. Just the four of us in a booth, awkwardly looking over the Cheddar's menu, trying to make the decision between the loaded baked-potato skins or the spinach artichoke dip. You know, the important decisions in life. (In case you're wondering, we chose the latter.) As soon as our orders were placed, the small talk abruptly ended, and the husband pulled a list out of his pocket and began to read all the offenses they had against us. That was bad enough…but then, suddenly the conversation turned to the topic of **my role** in the church. They shared a few specific instances of times they felt I had been too bold, or too assertive, or too…*whatever*.

Then, their words were pointed and direct as they looked straight into my eyes said,

> **"We can follow him as our pastor—but we can't follow you."**

I was stunned. I couldn't believe what I was hearing. These people were completely rejecting my influence in their lives. They refused to allow me to lead them. Not because I was unqualified. Not because I wasn't called. It was because I was a woman.

That moment broke me. I dismissed myself from the table and went to the ladies' room—because I definitely wasn't going to give them the satisfaction of seeing me cry. (*Remember the previous chapter? I'm just keeping it real.*)

My thoughts were running wild. *Who do these people think they are? Why didn't David jump in to defend me just now? Do other people in our congregation feel this way, too? What does this mean for my future? Do I not have a place in ministry of my own?*

I had followed the call of God since I was a junior high student. I had gone to Bible college — but honestly, there wasn't a clear path for women back then. There weren't many options. You could do kids ministry. Maybe go to the mission field. Or hopefully marry a pastor.

Suddenly, I wasn't sure where I fit.

I returned to the table, got through the meal, and we left. Needless to say, it was a quiet drive home that night. I was hurt and angry…but mostly confused.

I still knew God had called us to Austin—but I wasn't sure what my unique role would be. Interestingly, it was only a few months later that God opened a door of opportunity in my business—Arbonne. In the years that followed, it became both provision and preparation. For over a decade, that business not only sustained our family financially when the church couldn't, but it trained me in leadership. It built my confidence, developed my gifts, and even affirmed the call on my life when others wouldn't.

So please allow me to bring everything full circle.

Hopefully now you can better appreciate the gravity of that late-night conversation with David in the bedroom. This wasn't just a trivial disagreement; it was yet another defining moment. In 2005, I felt rejection. Now in 2018, I was asking the question once again, "Is there a place for me here?"

But this time, things would be different.

BETTER TOGETHER BECAME A MOVEMENT

When David (finally) shared our vision with the board, they immediately affirmed my new role. In fact, one of the board members told David, "We don't really see this as something new, at all; rather, it is just a recognition of what has already been happening. The two of you are a team—and our church family knows that. So now, we get to make it 'official.'"

Once they recognized me as *co-pastor*, everything changed. Not because the title somehow made us better—but because it brought clarity to our leadership model. What had been happening behind the scenes now became public, and our church family responded with enthusiasm. The shift was felt immediately, as both David and I flourished in ways neither of us expected. We shared the **work**, the **weight** and the **wins**. We embraced this new season with both humility and boldness. More of Him, less of us.

And what God began to pour into us, we committed to pour out.

We started seeing lonely leaders, isolated pastors, discouraged couples—just like we had been. And we realized our call wasn't just to build Bridge Church—it was to equip others. We saw the blueprint for multisite ministry. We began raising up kids' pastors, youth pastors, worship leaders, and campus pastors from within our house. We built teams. We coached leaders. We gave away every tool and lesson we had learned. We weren't building a brand—we were building the Kingdom.

It's been a long journey, but worth every step. God's timing is perfect. His plan is perfect. Not always clear. Not always fast. But perfect.

In the fullness of God's timing, here I am. Serving alongside my best friend. Leading an amazing church family. Grateful that we get to do this together.

And if I've learned anything—it's this: **You're not meant to do this alone.**

If you're married, lead together.
If you're single, link arms with mentors, spiritual siblings, and ministry family.
Build a team. Build a circle. Build the Kingdom.

Because *truly, deeply, joyfully*—**We are better together.**

PRACTICAL TAKEAWAYS

» **Say "Yes" Before You See the Whole Plan.**
God rarely gives us the full blueprint up front — He gives us just enough light for the next step. Say yes in faith; the clarity will come as you walk.

» **Lead** *With* **Your Spouse, Not Just Beside Them.**
If you're married, leadership is a shared space. Make time for honest check-ins. Talk about what's working, what's heavy, and how you can support each other better.

» **Cultivate a Spirit-Filled Inner Circle.**
Who are your five? The ones who shape your thoughts, prayers, and decisions? Choose voices that are wise, honest, godly, and full of the Spirit. It's okay to make adjustments.

» **Don't Lead Alone—Get a Coach or Mentor.**
Coaching isn't just for athletes—it's for leaders who want to grow. Don't wait for burnout. Find someone ahead of you who can guide, stretch, and speak life into your journey.

» **Give Away What You've Been Given.**
Leadership is multiplication. Every breakthrough, lesson, and testimony God has given you was meant to bless someone else. Who could you mentor or encourage right now?

» **Protect Your Marriage While You Build the Ministry.**
Ministry magnifies both the beautiful and the difficult. Stay connected. Set boundaries. Laugh more. Pray often. Your marriage is your first ministry—guard it well.

» **Champion Others as You Climb.**
Be the voice you once needed. Cheer loudly. Encourage freely. Whether it's women or men, open doors for others like Jesus opened them for you—freely and fully.

REFLECTION QUESTIONS

Use these for personal reflection, couple conversations, or your leadership circle.

1. **Where is God inviting you to say "yes" before all the pieces make sense?**

2. **Is there an insecurity—yours or someone else's—that might be limiting a God-ordained partnership?**

3. **Are the people closest to your calling helping you walk in freedom and truth? Who might need more or less access?**

4. **Have you been trying to carry leadership alone? Who could you invite into your rhythm this season?**

5. **Who is coaching or mentoring you right now—spiritually, practically, or both? Who could you ask to walk with you?**

6. **If you're married, how aligned are you and your spouse in ministry right now? What conversation needs to happen?**

7. **Who are you actively pouring into? What have you learned that someone else needs?**

8. **What would shift in your leadership if you truly lived out the truth: you're better together?**

BELIEVE FOR GREATER

"BOLD PRAYERS HONOR GOD, AND
GOD HONORS BOLD PRAYERS.
GOD ISN'T OFFENDED BY YOUR
BIGGEST DREAMS OR BOLDEST
PRAYERS. HE'S OFFENDED
BY ANYTHING LESS."
(MARK BATTERSON,
THE CIRCLE MAKER)

CHAPTER 6:
(DAVID:)

In chapter 3, we shared the story of our church's 80th anniversary celebration, which was held in 2018. In preparation for this celebration, our team pressed us for a theme. After all, like any good event planner knows, there must be a focal point—an inspiration that will guide decision-making on everything from printed invitations to table decorations.

So I asked for a few weeks to think (and pray) about it, but promised to get back to them. Opportunities like this don't exactly come around very often, so we wanted to host a celebration worthy of such a special occasion. The goal was two-fold: honor the past and look toward the future. Once I got quiet before the Lord, it didn't take long for Him to direct my heart to one particular passage of Scripture:

> 6 "This is what the Lord Almighty says: 'In a little while I will once more shake the heavens and the earth, the sea and the dry land. 7 I will shake all nations, and what is desired by all nations will come, and I will fill this house with glory,' says the Lord Almighty. 8 'The silver is mine and the gold is mine,' declares the Lord Almighty. 9 **'The glory of this present house will be greater than the glory of the former house**,' says the Lord Almighty. 'And in this place I will grant peace,' declares the Lord Almighty." (Haggai 2:6-9)

As I read verse 9, one word jumped out to me: **GREATER**. The glory of God in the past was great, but He promised that His glory in the future would be even greater. (*Sounded like the perfect verse for an 80th anniversary to me! Done.*) The more time I spent meditating on the promises found within this passage, the more excited my heart became.

So, as I've already shared, "GREATER" became the theme for our celebration. But this wasn't just a nice idea for the decorating team to run with—it felt like more than that. We began to sense it was a prophetic word over Bridge Church for the coming season. God was preparing us for greater influence, greater impact, and yes, greater responsibility. He was *stretching* us to believe for GREATER—and now, **we are believing the same for YOU!**

We are convinced God *wants* His Church to grow—and that includes the place where you serve. He *wants* the lost to be found! He is *for* you! He is ready and willing to show Himself faithful. In fact, this is our hope and prayer for you, for your family, and for your church or ministry:

Greater <u>fruitfulness</u>   …in your ministry

Greater <u>effectiveness</u>   …in your work

Greater <u>favor</u>   …in relationships

Greater <u>progress</u>   …in your goals

Greater <u>confidence</u>   …in your calling

Greater <u>vision</u>   …for your future

Greater <u>generosity</u>   …with your resources

Greater <u>influence</u>   …in your community

Greater <u>health</u>   …in your body

Greater <u>harvest</u>   …of souls – CHANGED LIVES!

Now, the only question is, *"Will you believe it?"*

FAITH OVER FEAR
(MICHELE:)

There's something sacred about this passage in Haggai. Every time David and I have had the opportunity to share it—pastor after pastor, missionary after missionary—you can feel the shift. Eyes fill with tears. Shoulders lift. Hearts lean in. Why? Because deep down, something awakens. **A holy expectancy. A whisper of hope. A flicker of faith that just maybe, God wants to do something greater.** Not just around them—but *in* them. *Through* them. In the very things their hands are touching.

And that promise? **"The glory of this present house will be greater than the glory of the former house."** That's not poetic nostalgia. That's prophetic declaration. God is not done. He's not dialing back His presence. He's pouring out more.

He is doing a *new thing*. But we must take Him at His Word. We have to believe—***really* believe**—that His glory is not fading, it's intensifying. That what's ahead of us is even more powerful than what's behind us. That what He's building right now in His Church is greater.

But here's a difficult reality: **Sometimes, the greater things of God can overwhelm or even intimidate us.** We want to believe His promises will be fulfilled—but if it happens, what exactly will that mean for us?

We start thinking:

> *"What would it be like if God really poured out his Spirit?"*

> *"What if God really answered our prayers?"*

> *"What if the GREATER THINGS are really ahead?"*

> *"Are we ready?!?"*

Can we be real with you for a minute? Sometimes fear is easier than faith. It's more comfortable. David and I totally understand what it means to have a scarcity mindset. We lived it for years. We have played it safe many times! We understand that fear secretly cripples your faith. Fear aborts dreams while they are still in the womb. Fear will lower your standards, shrink your expectations, and explain away your dreams.

Believe me, we know firsthand. We are preaching to ourselves, even now! But that's why we're writing this book. If you take away anything at all from our story, please let it be this:

We serve a God of abundance, *not* scarcity!

His Word says so. We're saying so. There is a cloud of witnesses in heaven who would absolutely say so! But the only thing that really matters is **what do YOU say?**

So before you read the rest of this chapter, take a moment to check your heart. Do you believe in a God who can (and will) keep His promises? If He called you, He *will* equip you. He *will* sustain you. He *will* protect you. He *will* provide for you. He *will* be faithful to His Word.

So, are *you* willing to believe for greater?

THE CHOICE IS YOURS

All of heaven awaits your answer. If the heroes of Scripture could speak to you right now, I bet at least a few of them would tell you to put your money where your mouth is!

Elijah asked God's people,

> *"How long will you waver between two opinions? If the Lord is God, follow him; but if Baal is God, follow him." (1 Kings 18:21)*

Joshua challenged the Israelites,

> *"Choose this day whom you will serve...but as for me and my house, we will serve the Lord." (Joshua 24:15)*

Always remember: This isn't about you anyway—so what is holding you back?

It's not about what you can do; it's about what God will do. It's not your church; it's God's church. It's not your reputation on the line; it's God's (and He's ok with that).

Today, right now as you're reading this, He is ready to do something GREATER in your life. You're not waiting on Him—He's waiting on you. Just listen to the words of the prophet Hanani, spoken to Asa, king of Judah:

> *"For the eyes of the Lord roam throughout the earth, so that He may strongly support those whose heart is completely His." (2 Chronicles 16:9 NASB)*

Isn't that a crazy thought? Just think, the eyes of the Lord are roaming about, looking for people whom He can support. Right now, God is looking for people whose hearts are fully committed to Him. People who need His help! People who He can trust. And when He finds them, He will show up in their lives in a big way!

So, again, are *you* willing to believe for greater?

If your answer is YES, keep reading.

(If not, we encourage you to put down this book and go spend some time talking to the One who called you. Ask Him to search your heart, to reveal what is holding you back from trusting Him fully. Don't rush it. Just listen, because there's no "next step" until you get this step right.)

FOUR QUESTIONS EVERY LEADER ASKS

Saying YES to God's call is always a great place to start—but remember, it's only the beginning. Whether planting a church, starting a new ministry, or just doing the next thing God asks of you—every step of faith comes with more uncertainty. It's an undeniable reality of spiritual leadership. That's just Faith 101. When God calls someone, He doesn't show them the full picture at once. His preferred approach is **little by little...until**.

Whenever God gives someone a vision, calling or assignment, there will always be four questions that come to mind. These are important questions that demand answers. We've asked them all. You probably have, too. But this passage in Haggai 2 reminds us God already has the answers...and He is more than willing to share with those who ask.

1. THE PEOPLE QUESTION: WHERE ARE THE PEOPLE GOING TO COME FROM?

When God gives a vision, it's totally natural for the leader to wonder,

> *"Where are the people going to come from? I can't do this alone, Lord. Who's going to help me?"*

REMEMBER: THIS ISN'T ABOUT YOU ANYWAY— SO WHAT IS HOLDING YOU BACK?

It's a natural—and necessary—question. Every pastor knows the weight of ministry, and no one can carry it alone. It's one thing to dream about leading a healthy, thriving church. It's another thing to realize that vision requires people to actually make it happen—faithful, called, servant-hearted people.

A healthy church needs greeters, ushers, hosts, worship leaders, singers, musicians, production volunteers, childcare workers, prayer partners—and yes, someone to make the coffee! Michele and I have had countless conversations with pastors and church leaders who feel like the entire ministry is riding on their shoulders. Some of them, to be honest, probably bring this on themselves, because of their own insecurity or need for control. (That's a subject for another book.) But many others are simply discouraged and exhausted—not because they don't want help, but because they don't know where the help is going to come from. The people question is real. It presses us to trust the One who calls people, raises up leaders, and sends people at the right time.

God's answer:

> In a little while I will once more shake the heavens and the earth, the sea and the dry land. I will shake the nations, and the desired of all nations will come (v.7)

Notice this: "The **desired** of all nations will come."

Can I tell you something? You don't want just *anyone*—you want the *right* ones. The ones God sends. The ones whose hearts beat for the same mission. The *desired* ones.

Don't waste time running around trying to convince anyone and everyone with a pulse to help you. Believe me, *you don't want the wrong people*. Those who bring their own agendas. Those who have competing priorities. Those who challenge the vision God has given you.

Michele puts it this way: **"Sometimes, rejection is God's protection."**

You don't just need *any* people to join your team—you need the *desired* people.

Here's the promise: **God will bring the PEOPLE.**

2.   THE PROVISION QUESTION: WHERE IS THE MONEY GOING TO COME FROM?

This question doesn't need much explanation (if any).

Every pastor and ministry leader has faced it—God gives a vision, and almost immediately the question follows:

How are we going to pay for this?

When vision expands, so do expenses. Buildings aren't cheap. Construction costs rise, utility bills pile up, insurance premiums increase, and maintenance is constant—and that's assuming your church even has a building.

On top of that, there's a passion to fund missionaries, send students to camp, serve the community, host outreach events, and even plant more churches. And everything—everything—costs money. It can feel overwhelming. At times, it's tempting to shrink the vision to fit the budget. After all, we only have so much, right? But the call of God has never been limited to the size of the bank account. The provision question is real—but so is the Provider. The challenge isn't whether God will supply; it's whether we will trust Him to do it in His way and His time. Faith doesn't ignore reality—it steps into it, believing that where God guides, He also provides.

God's answer:

> *"'The silver is mine and the gold is mine,' declares the Lord Almighty." (v.8)*

One of the most important lessons we've learned in ministry is this—**whatever God promises, He pays for.** He's got this. It's not your job to bankroll God's vision—it's His. He's a God of abundance, not scarcity, and He's never once run out of resources. Over and over again, we've watched Him provide exactly what we needed, often in ways we would've never predicted.

In December 2023, Michele was casually chatting with a friend, reflecting on how good God had been in recent years. 2022 had brought the miracle of the Foster Camp (shared in chapter 4). In 2023, out of nowhere, our church was randomly selected to be the host site for *Extreme*

Makeover: Home Edition, which was a cool opportunity to serve a local family in need. So, at the end of the year, Michele just asked a simple but faith-filled question: ***"I wonder what God is going to do next?"***

A KNOCK AT THE DOOR

(MICHELE:)

A week later, that question was answered. Late one afternoon, David and I were in his office when we heard a knock at the back door (something that never happens). When I opened the door, a man we did not recognize was standing there. When he asked if the church had a benevolence program, we assumed he was asking for himself. Surprisingly, he had come to make a donation—not ask for one. So he handed us two checks—one for a struggling family in the church, and one to use wherever needed.   It was a total God moment—right on time!

A year later (December 2025), we found ourselves in need once again. The cost of much-needed renovations at our SOCO Campus had been piling up quickly, so we felt it best to pause the project until more funds became available. (I'm a finisher, so this kind of stuff drives me crazy, by the way!). As we drove out of the SOCO parking lot, I remember praying the following words out loud (even though I was halfway joking):

> *"Lord, you know how badly we want to finish this remodel project...but we're almost out of money. So if you could just lay it on someone's heart to write a $100,000 check, that would be awesome! That would pay for everything...and more!"*

Two weeks later—on January 2, 2025—David and I needed to swing by the church to grab something from his office. While we were there, we took a minute to see if anything was in the mailbox. Sure enough, we found a plain white envelope with a handwritten check inside—the amount was enough to cover all remaining expenses of the SOCO project…and then some! Won't he do it?!?

These moments are more than stories—they're reminders. God provides when we pray specifically and trust boldly. Be specific and watch what God will do.
Here's the promise: **God will provide the money.**

3. THE PRESENCE QUESTION: IS GOD GOING TO BE WITH ME?

(DAVID:)

Every leader eventually wrestles with it:

Where is God in all of this? Will He be with us? Will He actually show up?

When the weight of ministry feels heavy or the future un-certain, we don't just need another strategy—we need the presence of God. What we need more than anything is not better programs, bigger budgets, or perfect plans—we need His glory. We need Him.

This is exactly what Moses understood in Exodus 33. When God told him, "My Presence will go with you, and I will give you rest" (v.14). Moses didn't just nod and move on. He pressed in deeper. He said, "*If your Presence does not go with us, do not send us up from here*" (v.15). That is the heart of a leader who knows what truly matters.

And God responded accordingly: "*I will do the very thing you have asked, because I am pleased with you and know you by name*" (v.17). What a promise! God sees you. He's pleased with you. He knows you by name. And He will go with you. So whatever challenge you are facing today, let this truth settle in your spirit—you are not alone. His presence is not just near you; it's within you. And because He's with you, everything is going to be okay.

God's answer:

> *"I will fill this house with glory..."* (v.7)
> *"The glory of this present house will be greater than the glory of the former house..."* (v.9)

Here's the promise: **God will send His PRESENCE.**

4.   THE PEACE QUESTION: IS THIS GONNA KILL ME?!?

After all the other questions are answered—the people show up, the provision comes through, and God's presence is near—there's still one question left:

> *Am I going to survive this?*
> *Is this going to be more than I can handle?*
> *Will I burn out, or give out, or pass out...?*
> *Am I going to have a nervous breakdown in the process?*

(OK, we're having a little fun with this one. Maybe a little over-the-top...but still true.)

Ministry is rewarding, but let's be honest—it's hard. It stretches you. It can wear you down. It's no wonder so many pastors battle discouragement. But God doesn't just send vision—He sends peace to carry it. He gives peace in the pressure, peace in the uncertainty, peace that surpasses understanding.

In Philippians 4:7, the apostle Paul describes this peace of God as something that *"guards your hearts and your minds in Christ Jesus."*

I love that word—*guard.* His peace isn't passive; it's protective. It surrounds your heart and mind when everything feels like it's falling apart. And if that weren't enough, Jesus Himself extends the invitation in Matthew 11:28—*"Come to* me, all you who are weary and burdened, and I will give you rest."

God's answer:

"And in this place I will grant peace," declares the Lord Almighty. (v.9)

Here's the promise:
God will send His PRESENCE.

So to every weary leader asking the peace question… Yes, it's hard. Yes, the pressure is real. But no, it won't break you. God promises His peace—and He always keeps His promises.

YES, IT'S HARD. YES, THE PRESSURE IS REAL. BUT NO, IT WON'T BREAK YOU.

REFLECTIONS ON THE JOURNEY

(MICHELE:)

Believing for GREATER often means stepping into something you can't fully see. But that's where God does His best work. That's where transformation begins. That's where we see clearly: it was never about us anyway.

It's all about more of Him and less of us.

When we look back at every major YES in our journey, we don't see perfect decisions or flawless faith. What we see is God's unwavering faithfulness. We see moments where we stumbled forward, unsure and afraid, only to find that He had already gone before us. And that gives us courage for the next YES.

We've lived it. Twenty years. An 85-year-old church. Our fifth location. Two building projects. A million reasons to quit—and one reason to keep going: **WE BELIEVE FOR GREATER.** Not because we're confident in ourselves. But because we're confident in Him.

Now, it's your turn.

BELIEVE FOR GREATER.

In your church. In your city. In your leadership. In your calling.

Take God at His word. Don't settle for surviving when He's called you to thrive. Don't replay the former glory when He's promised a greater one.

Say yes. Stick with it. Be real. Be faithful. Be bold.

He is shaking things so He can awaken things. He's growing His Kingdom. And He wants to use *you* to do it.

The invitation is still the same: Will you trust Me? Will you follow Me? Will you say YES?

Because on the other side of YES is where the real story begins—and it will be GREATER than you can ever dream on your own.

So if you're standing on the edge of a decision—a step that feels too risky, too unknown, too wild to make sense—know this: you are not alone. God is already in the middle of it. He is in the preparation. He is in the prompting. He is in the CRAZY.

ONE LAST THING:

If you will allow us, David and I would love to pray for God's GREATER over you.

As you read aloud the prayers below, please know we are agreeing with you right now. Amen

PRAYER FOR GREATER IN YOUR CHURCH:

Father, thank You for every shaking that has made room for Your glory. We ask You now—bring the right people. Release Your provision. Fill Your house with Your presence. And flood it with peace. Let the glory of this present Church outshine every former season. For Your Kingdom. For Your name. Amen.

PRAYER FOR GREATER IN YOUR LIFE:

Lord, I believe You have more. So I say yes—again. Stretch me.Shape me. Use me. Let me walk with faith, lead with courage, and love with boldness. I receive Your peace. I trust Your process. And I believe for greater—today, tomorrow, and until I see You face to face. Amen.

PRACTICAL TAKEAWAYS

» **Pray boldly and specifically.**

God doesn't answer vague prayers. (Mark Batterson). Bold prayers honor God because they reveal your trust in His power and provision.

» **Write down the vision.**

Clarify what "greater" means in your life, ministry, or next season. Journal or map out where you sense God is leading you and what that will require of you.

» **Shift your "scarcity mindset"**

Catch and replace any scarcity thoughts with Scripture (examples: Haggai 2:8 and Philippians 4:19). Speak life over your ministry, finances and calling.

» **Prioritize God's presence.**

Like Moses, determine not to move forward without His presence. Create daily space for worship, stillness and listening prayer.

» **Guard your peace.**

Recognize the warning signs of burnout and practice soul-care intentionally. Memorize Philippians 4:6-7 and declare it in anxious moments.

REFLECTION QUESTIONS

Use these for personal reflection, couple conversations, or your leadership circle.

1.   **Do I truly believe God wants to do something GREATER in and through me?**

2.   **What dreams or prayers have I considered "too bold" or "too unrealistic"?**

3.   **Am I functioning with a mindset of scarcity or abundance?** What lies am I believing about God's provision, presence or peace? Where have I seen God provide before?

4.   **Which of the four (4) leadership questions do I wrestle with the most right now?**

5.   **Have I been hesitant to say "yes" to something God is stirring in me? Why?** Is it timing, fear, doubt, or lack of clarity?

FINAL WORD: LET'S GO!

(US:)

So, there you have it.

This is our CRAZY story.

A story marked by chaos and calling—but always by God's presence in every twist and turn.

It's not a story about numbers, stats or spotlight moments. This is about what God is doing—He is building His Church. And we're simply grateful we get to see the fruit of it. The fruit of late nights, early prayers, honest conversations, hard seasons, and unwavering faith. We haven't arrived—and we never want to pretend we have. We're not special. We're not experts. We're just two people who said "yes" and kept saying it when things got hard. We are committed to keep learning. Keep growing. Keep stretching.

But this story has never been just about us.

It's a story of a church family that has walked this road together. A community of people who have let God shape us, stretch us, and structure us. We've learned the power of being real and authentic—because pretending doesn't set people free. And more than anything, we've learned this: **we are better together**. Not just us as a couple, but us as the Church. The pastors. The leaders. The everyday king-dom-builders. This is bigger than a building or a brand. It's about people meeting Jesus. That's the win.

We're watching people come alive in Christ. We're seeing hidden gifts come to the surface. People stepping into leadership—some for the first time. People discovering their purpose because someone finally stopped to say, "God's put something in you, and it matters." And that's what we're called to do as shepherds: help others find the purpose God planted inside them. We've seen new leaders emerge—youth pastors, kids pastors, worship pastors, connection pastors—you name it. And it never gets old.

This is our CRAZY story, and it's still unfolding. Yours is too.

So, today, we challenge you to…

SAY YES.

Even when you don't have the whole plan.

STICK WITH IT.

Even when it's hard.

LET GOD STRETCH AND SHAPE YOU.

Don't settle for safe.

BE REAL.

You don't need to be someone else. You just need to be who God created you to be.

WE ARE BETTER TOGETHER.

Call out the gold in others. Remind them: they don't have to do it alone. We are better together.

BELIEVE FOR GREATER.

No matter your church size, your team size, your past or your present—God has more. This isn't the end. He's not done with you. Don't live in a scarcity mindset when you serve a God of abundance.

Finally, this is our hope and prayer: If even one person finds one truth, one "aha" moment from this book and uses it to impact the Kingdom, we're forever grateful.

You got this.

God's got this.

LET'S GO! LET'S GO! LET'S GO!

ACKNOWLEDGEMENTS

To our Parents – Bob and Jackie Ledford, Jim and Nina McLain. – Thank you for your unwavering love, constant support, and the values you've instilled in us. Your prayers, encouragement and belief in us—especially during the hard seasons—have carried us more than you know.

To our Staff & Leadership Team (past and present) – For whatever time or season you served alongside us, we will forever be humbled and grateful for your YES. Your belief in us, and your unwavering support have meant more than words can express. We love you all!

To our Board (past and present) – Thank you for encouraging us to finally take this sabbatical—without that nudge, who knows when (or if) this book would have been finished. Thank you for your investment into our lives, and for standing with us as we continue to follow God's vision for this house.

Chris Sonksen – Thanks for being the world's greatest coach! (…and no, in case you're wondering, we don't say that to everyone!) Through many hours of blood, sweat and Celsius drinks, you've helped raise the bar of our leadership. From the beginning, you challenged us to take the leap and write this book—and here it is! Your wisdom and experience have helped us put the right structures in place to move the team—and the church—forward. Thanks for always being in our corner! We love you and Laura big time!

Jim and Becky Hennesy – Thank you for showing us a new way to do ministry as a couple. At least it was new to us, and we are grateful. Pastor Jim, we've probably never talked about that phone call—in fact, you may not even remember it—but I'm so thankful you made time for me that day. Your listening ear and matter-of-fact wisdom were what I needed. You and Becky are amazing leaders, and we are honored to call you friends.

Kerri Lofte – Thank you for walking this book-writing journey alongside us. Serving as both our financial secretary and executive assistant is no small task—especially with how much we can be! But your latest role of helping us edit this book? This officially makes you the G.O.A.T. We're so appreciative for your late nights, thoughtful input, and wise advice. You're simply the best!

The Man Who Knocked at the Back Door – You know who you are. Thank you for investing in the Kingdom, time and time again. Your generosity has helped accelerate the pace of the difference we're making—both around the block and around the world.

Lonnie Huett – Thanks for being sensitive enough to hear God's voice and faithful enough to obey it.   You were one of the CRAZIEST parts of this whole story…in more ways than one! Every single month, we tell new families in our church about that God-ordained conversation under the water tower. Bridge Church will forever be impacted by your YES, and generations will continue to hear about "a man named Lonnie."

Ken Rader – Thanks for all your sacrificial work on our first building—only the Lord truly knows what all you did when no one was looking. We've all heard the phrase "blood sweat and tears" – well, you almost gave your life, literally, putting up that pallet wall! Thank goodness for duct tape!

Cindy (Davis) Iverson – You and Todd were sent from God himself "for such a time as this." Thanks for the late nights laying carpet tiles, mopping floors, and only Heaven knows what else…. (Oh, and thanks for the Oakleys. I've still got them—Todd would be so proud.)

Brian Parker and Austin Coatings – Thanks for all the paint, not only with our two different building projects, but more recently with our SOCO Campus. We'll always be grateful for your dad, John Parker; his legacy is still bearing fruit in the Kingdom, even after all these years.

David Baze – Thanks for framing the walls, as well as installing all the cabinets and countertops. (I still remember those were some coooold mornings!) You and your guys were such a blessing. We may have another project for you…so let's talk soon!

Greg and Sandie Mundis – Thank you for inviting us to join you in Vienna for the Inspire gathering in 2018. We felt so honored to spend that time with you both. Little did we know how profoundly that week would alter the trajectory of our life and ministry. In the years that followed, your friendship has meant more than you know.

Melinda Henderson – (from Michele) Vienna 2018 was a "YES" I didn't see coming. God used your vision and your heart through Inspire to stir something deeper in me, calling me into a more intentional purpose back home in Austin. Thank you for your friendship, your obedience, and your relentless passion to see every girl know Jesus. I'm deeply grateful—and expectant for all that is still to come.

Larry Henderson – (from David) When I tagged along with Michele to Vienna in 2018, I just expected to carry her luggage and help serve the team. Never expected to make a new friend—but I did in you. Every time we get together, I walk away encouraged, challenged and inspired (yes, men should still be allowed to use that word, too). Still trying to find a time for that round of golf someday…maybe even in Scotland! Love you bro.

John and Tracy Houston – Thanks for blessing us with an unforgettable week in Vietnam. We still talk about that trip often. Your generous investment into a group of missions-minded pastors. Your words of wisdom about engaging intentionally with business leaders in our church.

Your contagious desire to make a Kingdom impact. And most of all, one random (Spirit-led) lunch conversation which confirmed God's new direction for our ministry together. Love y'all! Still gotta schedule our double-date at "Health Camp!"

Mike Powell – In 1997, when facing a pending transition in our ministry assignment, I shared that I was searching for an associate position; I assumed I needed one more opportunity to serve under a pastor who could mentor me. But one conversation with you got me thinking: "If you believe God has called you to be a pastor one day, don't wait until later. Do it now. Pray for God to open a door; then walk through it." A few months later, we were pastors of First Assembly of God in Van. TX. Thanks for challenging me to step out of my comfort zone and believe God for greater!

Roger Lewis – For over a decade, you led Central Assembly of God with integrity of heart and skillful hands. It was my honor to follow you, and your faithfulness provided a strong foundation for us to build upon. Not only were you the first one to tell me about the opportunity, but then once I became a candidate, you shared insights to help me make an informed decision. Thank you for setting us up to succeed and for always being an encourager—that kind of support from one's predecessor is not as common as it should be. You're a class act, always.

Charletta Garrison – Thank you for seeing me (Michele) when I was just a young junior high girl. You showed me that being my authentic self was enough—and that God could use me just as I am. Over the years, you've been a friend, mentor, encourager, counselor, traveling buddy, and even a workout partner. I'm standing on your shoulders today because of the love, wisdom and investment you poured into me. I'm forever grateful. Love you.

Robert McBride – When someone first meets their second-grade schoolteacher, I'm sure they never expect to become part of her family. That would be crazy right? But in your case, that's exactly what happened. For almost 30 years, in four different churches located in two states, you've continually been part of our lives. We've watched you grow as a husband, father, and follower of Jesus—and even had the privilege of baptizing you in water. We love you, Rylee and Ryker—and always remember how proud we are of you.

Bob Goodside – Thank you allowing us to establish our temporary "book-writing headquarters" in Galveston! Without your generous hospitality, there's no way we would have finished this project during our sabbatical. So glad you joined this CRAZY family!

Jade, Jonathon and our Grand-buddies, River and Arlo – Thank you for jumping into our wonderfully crazy family. We're honored to be your extended family, and it brings us so much joy to be Mimi and Mimu-Dave to those sweet boys who have completely stolen our hearts! We love you BIG, and we're so grateful to do life with you. (Oh, and if you want to keep the homemade salsa coming for the rest of our lives, we won't complain.)

Joseph & Jennifer Mena – You guys are amazing! Thanks for the countless conversations we've had through the years—laughing until our sides hurt, crying on each other's shoulders, and dreaming together about the future. Charter schools and church plants. Basketball games and backyard renovations. Prayer meetings and pool cleanings. Whatever life brings, you're always there. Seems like just yesterday, we were holding each other's newborn babies, now we are attending graduations…and even weddings! Inconceivable! (Speaking of weddings, who's next—Ethan or Ariana? Guess we'll find out soon enough…) Your family being OUR family is one of the greatest blessings in our lives. Still gotta figure out the details on this relocation to Austin…   Love you all!

Manny & Victoria Rivera – Thanks for being our "million dollar friends!" Always keep your passports current and a suitcase by the front door. Who knows when the phone will ring… We love traveling around the world doing missions stuff with you guys! Also, thanks for encouraging us to get this book done, and helping to make it happen. Love you both.

Eric & Trisha Porter — Our lives are better for your friendship. You've walked with us through many seasons of change and growth, and we've often been strengthened by your words of affirmation. (Not to mention, we've just laughed a lot!) Also, the influence of Backyard Orphans has left a lasting impact on our church community. We love you guys, and can't wait for our next beach trip…anywhere!

RECOMMENDED READING

For years, it has been our practice to read books together with our leadership team. We read a chapter or two each week, then discuss during our staff meetings. We expect them to come prepared to answer 2 questions, as they share:

1. What stood out the most about what you read, and why?

2. How will you apply this to your life and/or leadership this week?

Then everyone shares. Everyone. It has often been said that "leaders are readers" – therefore, we are always striving to strengthen this discipline within our team culture. Since we are often asked which books have been most beneficial, we thought it would be a good idea to share a list of our favorites. Hope you enjoy them as much as we did!

Mark Batterson

1. The Circle Maker

2. Win The Day

3. Do It For a Day

Patrick Lencioni

1. The Ideal Team Player

2. The Five Dysfunctions of a Team

3. The Advantage

4. The Motive

Chris Sonksen

1. Saving Your Church From Itself
2. When Your Church Feels Stuck
3. Traction

Jon Gordon

1. The Energy Bus
2. The No Complaining Rule
3. Training Camp

Various Authors

1. The Church of Irresistible Influence – Robert Lewis
2. Love Does – Bob Goff
3. Prodigal God – Timothy Keller
4. The Dream Giver – Bruce Wilkinson
5. The Principle of the Path – Andy Stanley
6. Soul Keeping – John Ortberg
7. The Power of Moments – Chip and Dan Heath
8. At Your Best – Carey Nieuwhof
9. Culture Code – Daniel Coyle
10. Anonymous – Alicia Britt Chole
11. Win In The Dark – Joshua Medcalf and Luca Jadin
12. Praying Like Fools, Living Like Monks – Tyler Staton
13. A Tale of Three Kings: A Study in Brokenness – Gene Edwards

ABOUT THE AUTHORS

David & Michele McLain live in Round Rock, Texas, just north of Austin. Married for 31 years and in ministry together for just as long, they have faithfully served as pastors at Bridge Church for the past 21 years. Together, they've raised four daughters— Madison, Macy, Mackenzie, and Madelyn. David is especially excited to have some more men in the family with the addition of their two son-in-laws, Cadyn and Josh. They are also thrilled to be grandparents to their first grandson, Lincoln James.

David and Michele are passionate about the local church. They deeply love pastors and are committed to raising up the next generation of leaders. Their heart is to encourage, equip, and invest in others, believing that healthy leadership makes a difference.